CAMPAIGN • 229

KOHIMA 1944

The battle that saved India

ROBERT LYMAN

ILLUSTRATED BY PETER DENNIS

Series editor Marcus Cowper

OSPREY PUBLISHING
Bloomsbury Publishing Plc

Kemp House, Chawley Park, Cumnor Hill, Oxford OX2 9PH, UK
29 Earlsfort Terrace, Dublin 2, Ireland
1385 Broadway, 5th Floor, New York, NY 10018, USA
Email: info@ospreypublishing.com
www.ospreypublishing.com

OSPREY is a trademark of Osprey Publishing Ltd

First published in Great Britain in 2010
Transferred to digital print in 2023

A catalogue record for this book is available from the British Library.

Print ISBN: 978 1 84603 939 3

Editorial by Ilios Publishing Ltd, Oxford, UK – www.iliospublishing.com
Page layout by The Black Spot
Index by Mike Parkin
Maps by www.bounford.com
Battlescene illustrations by Peter Dennis
Typeset in Sabon and Myriad Pro
Originated by PDQ Media
Printed and bound in India by Replika Press Private Ltd.

24 25 26 27 28   12 11 10 9 8 7

The Woodland Trust
Osprey Publishing supports the Woodland Trust, the UK's leading woodland conservation charity.

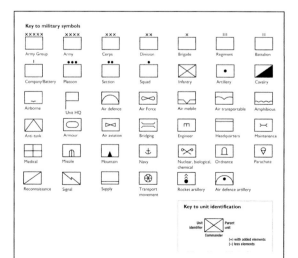

Dedication

This book is dedicated to the memory of Jon Latimer, whose death at the age of 44 took from us, in 2009, a skilful and perceptive historian. Jon's book on the war in the Far East remains by far the best single volume on what is often called 'The Burma Campaign'. This book should have been written by him.

When you go home
Tell them of us
And say, for your tomorrow
We gave our today

Epitaph on the 2nd Division Memorial, Kohima

Acknowledgements

In the writing of this book special thanks are extended to Philip, Isla and Ben Brownless, Smo and Lily Das, David and Rosemary Murray, Gordon and Betty Graham, Rob and Sylvia May, Jerry Bird, Colonel Ted Shields, Bob Cook, Pfelie Kesiezie, Peter Toole, Thomas Joesbury, Stanley Hutson, Kenneth Keen, Len Hall, Ray Jackson, Clifford Wood, C. V. (Mike) Ball, Wilf Ogden, John Skene MBE, Roy Welland, Bob Allen, Alex Tiller, Brigadier John Randle OBE MC, Colonel Donald Easten MC and Raymond Street.

For material in the BBC Peoples War Archive I wish to thank Fred Weedman (A5325518) and Bob Blenkinsop (A2052181). For permission to quote from material in the Department of Documents and the Sound Archives at the Imperial War Museum in London I am grateful to copyright holders of material by Pat Rome MC (DS/MISC/65) and John Howard (99/21/1).

In the sound archives can be found dramatic, first-hand descriptions of the battles including those by John Randle (15335, 20457); F. G. Nields (MAPC); John Winstanley (17955); Francis Boshell (15578); Martin McLane (10165); Alexander Wilson (20456); Sam Horner; William Robinson (17667); 'Winkie' Fitt (16970); Dick Fiddament (17354); Maurice Franses (17353); Walter Gilding (17534); Dickie Davies (17936); Henry Cook (17265) and Lintorn Highett (15334). Ian Kikuchi and his team in the Department of Film at the IWM were unfailingly generous in their support. I am particularly grateful also to the hard work of David Percy in securing the photographs from the shaky combat cinematography of the time.

Artist's note

The illustrations are dedicated to the memory of Derek Tomlinson, my father-in law, who fought at Kohima and in all the battles of the Forgotten Army.

Readers may care to note that the original paintings from which the colour plates in this book were prepared are available for private sale. The Publishers retain all reproduction copyright whatsoever. All enquiries should be addressed to:

Peter Dennis, Fieldhead, The Park, Mansfield, NOTTS, NG18 2AT, UK

The Publishers regret that they can enter into no correspondence upon this matter.

Imperial War Museum collections

Many of the photos in this book come from the Imperial War Museum's huge collections which cover all aspects of conflict involving Britain and the Commonwealth since the start of the twentieth century.

These rich resources are available online to search, browse and buy at www.iwmcollections.org.uk. In addition to Collections Online, you can visit the Visitors Rooms where you can explore over 8 million photgraphs, thousands of hours of moving images, the largest sound archive of its kind in the world, thousands of diaries and letters written by people in wartime, and a huge reference library.

To make an appointment call: (020) 7416 5320.
Or email: mail@iwm.org.uk
Imperial War Museum: www.iwm.org.uk

www.ospreypublishing.com

To find out more about our authors and books visit our website. Here you will find extracts, author interviews, details of forthcoming events and the option to sign-up for our newsletter.

CONTENTS

THE ORIGINS OF THE CAMPAIGN

THE JAPANESE IN BURMA

The conquest of Burma in May 1942 brought the Japanese Army to India's eastern border. During 1943 the idea of entering India itself began to take shape although a plan to do this by advancing north through the Hukawng Valley and then falling on Assam down the Brahmaputra Valley from Ledo – Operation *21* – was rejected as impracticable. North-eastern India (the provinces of Assam and Manipur) was important to the Allies as the American base for the provision of supplies to Nationalist Chinese forces via airlift operations over 'The Hump' (the mountainous region between India, Burma and China) and because it provided the point of departure (from Imphal, capital of Manipur in eastern Assam) for any British land offensive into Burma. Indeed, in May 1943 a limited offensive by 3,000 men of Brigadier Orde Wingate's 'Chindits' had crossed from Imphal, over the Chindwin and deep into Japanese-held Burma. There, for three months, they had caused themselves a nuisance to the Japanese by attacking roads and railway lines, worrying the Japanese that further and more substantial operations might follow to threaten their hegemony in Burma.

In late 1943 the Japanese command in Burma was reorganized, and a new headquarters, Burma Area Army, was created under the command of Lieutenant-General Kawabe Masakasu. One of its subordinate formations, responsible for the central part of the front facing Manipur, was the Fifteenth Army whose new commander, Lieutenant-General Mutaguchi Renya, was impressed by the apparent success of Wingate's expedition. Initially a strong opponent of Operation *21* he became persuaded of the need to launch an offensive into India. Throughout the latter half of 1943 he lobbied shamelessly across the Burma Area Army for permission to do so. He argued that at the very least the occupation of Imphal (the capital of Manipur and the location of the British IV Corps) would prevent the British attempting to repeat their offensive into Burma on a larger scale. In this he was supported from an unlikely source. Following the collapse of British resistance in Malaya and Singapore in 1942 large numbers of Indian soldiers had fallen into Japanese hands, 16,000 eventually forming the Indian National Army (INA). The political leader of this movement – Subhas Chandra Bose – argued that with the INA in the vanguard of an offensive into India it might even topple the Raj, by setting off an unstoppable conflagration of anti-British sentiment among the native population. Mutaguchi eagerly grasped such ideas as further justification for an offensive.

An ambulance driving through Kohima on the road up to Naga Village. This part of the high ground between Treasury Hill and Naga Hill saw little direct fighting, but remained in Japanese possession until early June. Many of the ambulance drivers were members of the American Field Service, men who earned the admiration of their Indian and British colleagues for their courage and selfless dedication to duty. (IWM, Ind 3447)

So it was that in March 1944, when on every other front the Japanese were on the strategic defensive, Japan launched a vast, audacious offensive (Operation C) deep into India with the entire 115,000-strong Fifteenth Army. Mutaguchi had got his way, persuading Kawabe in turn to request permission for the offensive from Field Marshal Count Terauchi, commander of the Southern Army in Saigon and ultimately Prime Minister Tojo in Tokyo. Kawabe gave detailed orders in turn to Mutaguchi on 19 January 1944. The commander of Fifteenth Army was instructed to mount a strong pre-emptive strike against Imphal before the onset of the monsoon in May. To help, a strong diversionary attack was planned for Arakan (Operation Z) a month before. If Lieutenant-General 'Bill' Slim, commander of the British Fourteenth Army, was deceived into thinking that this was the focus of an offensive against India, and moved his strategic reserves to deal with it, Operation Z would have done its duty, allowing Mutaguchi the best possible odds in Manipur. At the same time aggressive Japanese operations in the Hukawng Valley would also prevent interference in Operation C by Lieutenant-General 'Vinegar Joe' Stilwell's Chinese.

THE BRITISH IN ASSAM AND MANIPUR

Eastern India was defended in 1944 by Slim's Fourteenth Army which, when first constituted in August 1943 (from the old pre-war 'Eastern Army'), had two corps. The first, XV Corps under the command of Lieutenant-General Philip Christison, was responsible for Arakan and the second, IV Corps under the command of Lieutenant-General Geoffrey Scoones, was responsible for the defence of Assam and Manipur. With its HQ in Imphal, IV Corps had about 30,000 troops in three Indian infantry divisions, together with an independent tank brigade. The 17th Indian Division lay far to the south of Imphal in the Chin Hills around Tiddim, the 20th Indian Division at Tamu on the Chindwin while the 23rd Indian Division and the 254th Tank Brigade were in reserve at Imphal. This was the largest number of troops that the long and difficult line of communication back to Dimapur could sustain without reliance on air supply. In early 1944 IV Corps was slowly preparing to launch its own limited offensive over the Chindwin and into Burma and therefore was not positioned to receive one coming the other way.

KOHIMA

Between Manipur and the Brahmaputra Valley lie the Naga Hills, covering some 20,000 square kilometres (8,000 square miles) of twisted, jungle-covered hills, the principal town of which is Kohima, sitting at 1,500m (5,000ft) above sea level. The entire region boasted few roads and a scattered aboriginal population of perhaps 200,000 people, with a significant population grouping at Kohima, through which ran the road between Dimapur (in the Brahmaputra Valley, also known as 'Manipur Road') and Imphal, a distance of 222km (138 miles). It was upgraded to a twin-track metalled road after many months of exhausting work in early 1943, but it still took a jeep some seven hours to travel between Imphal and Dimapur. It was also subject to regular mudslides and during the monsoon (between May and October) found itself regularly closed to traffic while repairs were undertaken. The people who inhabited this vast hill country were the Nagas, an animistic race largely converted to Christianity after the arrival of American missionaries in the 19th century.

At Dimapur a vast array of depots was being constructed to supply Stilwell's forces beyond Ledo and those of IV Corps across the mountains to Imphal.

There are three dominant physical features in the Kohima area. As the road completes the final approach after its 74km (46-mile) journey from Dimapur it rises to meet the Kohima Ridge, on which a range of supply depots, and the Deputy Commissioner's bungalow, were situated. At Zubza, 16km (10 miles) before reaching Kohima, one can stand and look up the valley towards the Kohima Ridge towering in the distance, 600m (2,000ft) higher in altitude. Between Zubza and Kohima the valley narrows rapidly, the ridge on the left running from Merema all the way to Naga Village, both sides ending in a bottleneck at the Kohima Ridge.

The northern edge of the ridge itself (called 'Summerhouse' or Garrison Hill) is thickly wooded, the slopes on the extreme left-hand edge, around which the road skirts, is the site of the 53rd Indian General Hospital (IGH) Spur. The slopes leading up to the ridge from the valley floor at this point are savagely abrupt and covered in thick jungle. At the left-hand (northern) edge of the ridge the road bifurcates at the Traffic Control Point (TCP). The left-hand fork takes the road across Treasury Ridge and up a broad hill – commonly called Naga Hill – atop of which lies Naga Village. At the TCP the right-hand fork takes the road around the eastern edge of the Kohima Ridge in the direction of the slopes of Mount Pulebadze (2,293m [7,522ft]), behind which sits Mount Japfü. The distance as the crow flies between Naga Hill on the left, and Mount Pulebadze on the right, is 3km (2 miles). Running east–west on Naga Hill side is a long ridge, with the village of Merema at the western end. Possession of the Naga Hill–Merema ridge allows observation of the northern edge of Kohima Ridge and the road, on the opposite side of the valley, twisting and turning through the hills from Dimapur.

Kohima is of considerable geographical significance because the ridge provides a natural block in the mountains between Manipur in the east and the Brahmaputra Valley in the west. If the Kohima Ridge could be blocked, access for any invader would be greatly reduced. In 1944 the ridge was home to the scattered support depots and stores necessary to sustain a small peacetime garrison on the road to Imphal. Charles Pawsey MC, the Deputy Commissioner for Nagaland since 1935 and a veteran of the Western Front, lived in a bungalow on the northernmost slopes, the driveway to his house slipping down the hill to touch the main Imphal–Dimapur road at the Traffic Control Point (TCP). To provide some leisure facilities a tennis court had been built above his bungalow. Overlooking the entire ridge from the south-eastern end was a distinctive pimple known as Jail Hill, named after the local prison that lay at its base. The highest point of the ridge was Kuki Piquet.

As one approaches from Dimapur the first point of high ground reached is Jotsoma, 3km (2 miles) from Kohima and enjoying a clear view of the ridge. Leaving the road and heading up the hillside to the right a stiff three-hour climb carries one to the top of Mount Pulebadze. Behind Pulebadze a track crosses the saddle over to the top of Aradura, and spurs flow down northwards into the eastern side of Kohima. In the foothills of these spurs sit, among other landmarks, the deeply forested Congress Hill and General Purpose Transport (GPT) Ridge, all of which offer sight of and dominate, Kohima Ridge from the south. There was virtually no part of the ridge that was not dominated in some way by another feature, or could not be fired at or observed from elsewhere. It could easily be surrounded (although the western slope was extremely steep), and without water could not hold out for long. In fact, it was, in conventional terms, indefensible. Because of this no thought had been given to its protection.

CHRONOLOGY

3 March Japanese 33rd Division begin their advance towards Tiddim, a week earlier than expected.

15 March On the day that intelligence predicted, the 15th and 31st Divisions cross the Chindwin, the 31st Division en route for Kohima.

19 March The lead battalions of the 31st Division surprise the unprepared, understrength and ill-equipped 50th Indian Parachute Brigade at Sheldon's Corner.

20 March 161st Brigade (5th Indian Division) flown into Dimapur from Arakan to reinforce Kohima.

21 March 50th Indian Parachute Brigade manages to converge on a new defensive position at Sangshak.

22 March Mass Japanese attacks begin against Sangshak.

Slim orders a scratch garrison to assemble at Kohima under Colonel Hugh Richards.

26 March The remnants of 50th Indian Parachute Brigade evacuate the Sangshak positions. The much-weakened 31st Division continues its delayed advance towards Kohima.

27 March Slim asks Giffard for the 2nd Division to be diverted from its intended destination – Arakan – and sent to Dimapur, for the defence of Kohima, instead.

29 March Imphal–Kohima road cut at Milestone 72, and Imphal besieged.

Brigadier Warren of 161st Brigade arrives in Kohima.

1 April First elements of 2nd Division arrive in panic-stricken Dimapur.

3 April General Stopford's HQ XXXIII Corps set up at Jorhat.

Royal West Kents ordered to withdraw from Kohima and defend Dimapur instead.

4 April First exhausted elements of 31st Division arrive in Kohima.

5 April Royal West Kents rushed back to occupy positions on Kohima Ridge, digging in under Japanese fire.

6 April Coordinated Japanese attacks fall on the defended perimeter of Kohima Ridge.

8 April 138th Regiment cut Kohima Ridge off from the 161st Brigade HQ and gun positions at Jotsoma.

138th Regiment instructed by Mutaguchi to continue their advance on Dimapur.

9 April	Lance-Corporal John Harman wins a posthumous VC on DIS (Daily Issue Store) Hill.	23 April	Final Japanese attempt to overwhelm Garrison Hill fails. Thereafter, Sato turns to the defensive.
	Patrol of the 7th Worcesters 'bumps' a Japanese patrol at Zubza.	25 April	4th Brigade begins its march behind Mount Pulebadze.
10 April	DIS Hill abandoned, and perimeter shortened.	27 April	Entire 5th Brigade in position on Merema Ridge.
	Monsoon rains begin early (they were expected in May).		Lee Grant tanks join 5th Brigade on Naga Hill after fighting their way through the TCP and across Treasury Ridge.
11 April	Arrival of 2nd Division in Dimapur complete.	29 April	4th Brigade ordered to cut short its flanking march, and cross Pulebadze to fall on GPT from above.
	7th Worcesters attack 'Bunker Hill' at Zubza but are repulsed.		
14 April	1st Cameron Highlanders, supported by overwhelming artillery support, destroy small Japanese force on 'Bunker Hill'.	30 April	Sato sends a signal to Mutaguchi saying that the 31st Division was at the end of its endurance.
	A patrol of the 4/7th Rajputs make it through the perimeter from Jotsoma.	1 May	4th Brigade occupies Oaks Hill.
16 April	2nd Division and 161st Brigade troops join hands at Jotsoma.	4 May	Royal Norfolks clears topmost part of GPT Ridge.
17 April	Japanese capture FSD (Field Supply Depot) Hill and Kuki Piquet.		161 Brigade clears Two Tree Hill.
18 April	Kohima Garrison reached for first time by troops from Jotsoma, including Lee Grant tanks.		First toehold secured on FSD Hill by Durhams on Kohima Ridge.
	First battalion of 5th Brigade crosses the Zubza nullah to cut the Merema–Bokajan Road.		5th Brigade seizes Church Knoll and Hunters Hill after bypassing Japanese positions on Merema Ridge.
	Sato ordered by Mutaguchi to send troops to the support of 15th Division attempting to break into Imphal.	6 May	In successfully clearing southernmost positions on GPT Ridge Captain Jack Randle awarded a posthumous VC.
20 April	Kohima Garrison relieved by troops of the 2nd Division.		Newly arrived 33rd Indian Brigade begins replacing British 6th Brigade on Kohima Ridge.
	Sato complains to HQ Fifteenth Army that none of the promised supplies has arrived.	11 May	4th Brigade finally clears GPT Ridge.
		12 May	FSD Hill cleared by men of the Royal Berkshires.

3 May	Dorsets finally clear DC's bungalow on Garrison Hill, after Lee Grant tanks manage to climb onto the tennis court.	28 May	Attacks by British 6th Brigade on Aradura Spur fail.

3 May — Dorsets finally clear DC's bungalow on Garrison Hill, after Lee Grant tanks manage to climb onto the tennis court.

5 May — Treasury Hill secured, as men of the 5th Brigade join up with those of 33rd Brigade.

Attack by Cameron Highlanders to secure Hunter's Hill fails.

9 May — Further deliberate attack on Hunter's Hill also fails.

3 May — 7th Indian Division takes responsibility for Naga Hill.

Sato exhorts his men to fight to the last.

5 May — Sato asks Mutaguchi for permission to withdraw but is refused.

28 May — Attacks by British 6th Brigade on Aradura Spur fail.

4/1st Gurkhas infiltrate Japanese positions on Hunter's Hill and finally take the position.

31 May — Sato orders his division to withdraw from Kohima.

3 June — Japanese fall back from Aradura Spur and begin defended withdrawal.

22 June — Troops of the 2nd Division from Kohima, and the 5th Indian Division advancing up from Imphal, meet at MS 108. The siege of Imphal is over.

OPPOSING COMMANDERS

Lieutenant-General Mutaguchi Renya, commander of the Japanese Fifteenth Army which launched its invasion of India in March 1944. Mutaguchi had hoped that Kohima would be quickly seized, which would allow Sato's 31st Division to sweep down into the Brahmaputra Valley and instigate an Indian uprising against the Raj. He was to be disappointed. Sato did not make much effort to push on to Dimapur, wasting a valuable opportunity to destroy the nodal point of all British counter effort in the Naga Hills and into Manipur, and then was halted by the spirited defence of the Kohima Ridge. (Author's collection)

JAPANESE COMMANDERS

General Kawabe Masakazu became commander of the newly formed Burma Area Army, based in Rangoon, in 1943. Kawabe reported to Field Marshal Count Terauchi, commander of the Southern Army, which was based in Saigon. The commander of Operation C, based on Fifteenth Army – part of Kawabe's Burma Area Army – was **Lieutenant-General Mutaguchi Renya** who had made his name commanding the 18th Division in the capture of Singapore in February 1942. He had an irrepressible, optimistic and excitable personality. His considerable emotional and physical appetites, especially for women and alcohol were legendary in the Imperial Japanese Army (IJA), as was his gung-ho militarism, which brooked no patience with any policy that did not support the glorification of Japan and the furtherance of her interests by force if necessary. He was not an intellectual, and was ruled in all things by his heart rather than his head. A committed militarist he was mentally and emotionally transfixed by the concept of *bushido,* allowing its myths to shape his personality and ambitions, believing in it as fervently as the fanatical adherent of any literalist religious sect.

From his earliest days as a soldier Mutaguchi's personal bravery, courage and contempt for death had created an uneasy relationship with those whom he commanded. They did not love him, but his dynamism and aggressive leadership nevertheless generated considerable respect. The truth was that he was a glory-hunter, and the lives of his men were incidental to his achievement of military fame. Unfortunately, his men knew this. But his single greatest personal failing was his inability to engender loyalty amongst his subordinate commanders. His bombast and bullying created enemies amongst men whom he urgently needed on his side, and created a climate of fear in his own headquarters, where officers, worried about the abuse they would receive, were fearful of giving him unpalatable information.

Kawabe believed that he would be an ideal commander for this offensive but was concerned that Mutaguchi would take too many risks, particularly in attempting to take his army into the Brahmaputra Valley, which was beyond the remit of his instructions. Kawabe had been Mutaguchi's immediate superior in China in 1937, when the latter had been at the centre of the machinations that had led to the expansion of the Sino-Japanese War, and knew him well. He was convinced that he could control Mutaguchi, and keep him within the limits that had been agreed, believing that Mutaguchi's single-mindedness made it more rather than less likely that the operation would succeed.

The commander of the 31st Division, one of Mutaguchi's three divisions, and responsible for the capture of Kohima, was **Lieutenant-General Sato**. Sato's reputation in the IJA was as a sound, somewhat plodding and unimaginative commander, but a determined and aggressive one nevertheless. On the face of it he appeared the ideal man to lead the advance against Kohima. But he had long been a political enemy of Mutaguchi and this underlying belligerence made him a difficult, if not impossible, subordinate. Even worse, Sato disliked Mutaguchi intensely. The events of the struggle at Kohima were to bring his hatred of the army commander into public view and were to result in Sato's deliberately and directly disobeying Mutaguchi's explicit instructions. The 31st Division also had a commander of its divisional infantry, **Lieutenant-General Miyazaki Shigesaburo**. Each of Sato's three regiments (the equivalent of a British brigade, each comprising three battalions) was commanded by a colonel, respectively **Colonel Fukunaga** (58th Regiment), **Colonel Torikai** (138th Regiment) and **Colonels Miyamoto** (KIA) and **Hirunuma** (124th Regiment).

The commander of the Army Air Force in Burma in 1944, supporting Operation C, was **Major-General Tazoe Noburu**. The political leader of the Indian National Army in 1944 was **Subhas Chandra Bose**, an exiled radical Bengali Congress party leader who was militant and charismatic. In July 1943 Bose persuaded Kawabe that a Japanese invasion of even a small part of India – suitably propagandized as a 'March on Delhi' designed to free India from the oppression of the British Raj – would spark an unstoppable nationalist bushfire across the whole of India. Persuaded by Bose's passion, Kawabe told the Indian nationalist that when the time came the INA would be allocated a leading role in an operation.

BRITISH COMMANDERS

Lieutenant-General Bill Slim was one of the pre-eminent soldiers of his generation. He was promoted to temporary command of the Eastern Army in August 1944 at a time when British fortunes in the Far East were at their lowest ebb (his predecessor had been sacked). Tough, wise, accessible to all he was the epitome of the great commander. Against the most formidable of obstacles, he helped to transform Allied fortunes in Burma such that profound defeat in 1942 was turned into overwhelming and comprehensive victory in 1945.

Lieutenant-General 'Bill' Slim Commander of the British Fourteenth Army that decisively destroyed Mutaguchi's Fifteenth Army in its 'March on Delhi' in the Naga Hills and Manipur between March and July 1944. (Alamy, B4WF4J)

Lieutenant-General Sir Montagu Stopford, GOC XXXIII Indian Corps, which was brought in to help the British 2nd Division retake the Kohima area from Sato's tenacious 31st Division. (IWM, SE1800A)

Slim's great success lay in understanding what it would take to defeat the Japanese in battle, and what he needed to do to his army to achieve this objective, which in 1943 seemed impossibly far off. In addition to developing a strategy for defeating Mutaguchi's offensive in 1944, Slim worked from first principles in 1943 to transform the morale and motivation of his men, Indian (predominately), Gurkha and British. He did this so spectacularly that by the end of the desperate battles against the Japanese in 1944 Slim had become 'Uncle Bill', a sobriquet soon in universal currency in Fourteenth Army, and which was to remain with him for the rest of his days.

In October 1943 when Slim's command of the Eastern Army was confirmed and renamed the Fourteenth Army it had two corps, IV Corps in Assam under the command of **Lieutenant-General Geoffrey Scoones**, and XV Corps in northern Arakan commanded by **Lieutenant-General Philip Christison**.

Lieutenant-General Montagu Stopford commanded the Fourteenth Army Group reserve – XXXIII Corps – which was drawn in to take the lead in the relief of the siege of Kohima. At the time the battle for Kohima broke in April 1944 its two divisions were the British 2nd Infantry Division, commanded by **Major-General John Grover** and the 7th Indian Infantry Division commanded by **Major-General Frank Messervy**. The 161st Indian Infantry Brigade, originally part of 5th Indian Division and the lone initial defender of the Kohima Ridge, was commanded by **Brigadier 'Daddy' Warren** and attached to XXXIII Corps on the latter's arrival in Assam in early April.

Messervy was known to his men – Indian, Gurkha and British – as 'Uncle Frank' and was highly regarded by them as a bold and inspirational leader. His dash and drive in Arakan in early 1944 had impressed Slim greatly, and he went on to very successful corps command in late 1944 and 1945. Grover was also well liked by his men, although he was a demanding disciplinarian. However, Grover was unfairly criticized by Slim and Stopford for the slowness of his division's advance through Kohima in April through to June 1944, and was relieved from his post – to the great anger of his men – at the moment victory was attained. During the fighting for Kohima the 2nd Division suffered high losses of its brigadiers, all of whom were aggressive, fighting commanders. Its brigade commanders were, successively, **Brigadier Goschen** (KIA); **Brigadier Theobalds** (KIA) and **Acting Brigadier Robert Scott** (WIA) in 4th Brigade; **Brigadier Hawkins** (WIA) in 5th Brigade and **Brigadier Shapland** (WIA) in 6th Brigade.

OPPOSING FORCES

JAPANESE FORCES

The basis of Japanese soldiers' remarkable fighting ability was the survival through long years of war of the *bushido* code of the ancient knightly samurai caste which defined, almost religiously, the life, purpose, motivations and ultimately the death of the Japanese soldier. Loyalty to the monarch was an inviolable spiritual and moral duty for all soldiers. The ultimate purpose of a samurai was not merely obedience, but death. Disobedience, disloyalty or failure was inconceivable. All professional soldiers of the time included in their daily routine obeisance to the emperor, through a ritual and energetic '*banzai!*' ('May the emperor live for 10,000 years!'), bowing in prayer in the direction of Tokyo. The *bushido* code entailed a commitment – philosophical,

Japanese infantry en route to Kohima. The Japanese achievement in marching over some of the most inhospitable terrain on earth, carrying all they needed for the impending battle, was considerable. Not for the first time in the war British commanders, who could not conceive that their lines of communication would be threatened by foot-borne Japanese infantry marching 190km (120 miles) from the Chindwin, were taken by surprise. (Topfoto, 904889)

intellectual, intensely practical and even religious – to a set of obligations tha led inevitably to death in the service of a heroic ideal. These obligations wer enshrined by Tojo in the 'Soldier Code' issued in 1941, and obliged the tru samurai to die in the service of his country and emperor, rather tha surrender, which was despised as the route of the coward and scoundrel.

It appeared to many Indian and British troops in 1942 and 1943 that new type of warfare and a new type of enemy had engulfed them. Tough frugal and determined, the Japanese were far better prepared and equippe for a savage jungle-based war than the British and Indian soldiers wh opposed them. Japanese tactics copied those of the European blitzkrieg idea designed above all to achieve shock and paralysis in their enemy. In this the proved to be resoundingly successful. The seemingly inaccessible jungle, place of fear for many British and Imperial troops, was used extensively fo movement. Commanders sought routinely to disrupt and confuse thei enemy. Roads and headquarters were attacked in order to paralyze Britis command and control arrangements, overload commanders and caus confusion among the troops. The Japanese had a particular penchant fo emerging from the jungle far to the rear of a main position and settin up roadblocks on the all-important lines of communication upon whic the British relied for movement and supplies. By infiltrating behind an through British defensive positions, they made the defenders believe tha they were cut off with no hope of escape, and by moving quickly throug thick jungle to appear far behind the 'front line' they induced panic. The moved quickly and lightly, unencumbered with the scales of transport an *matériel* of war that characterized the British. At the outset of the war the Japanese were amazed at the ease with which they could psychologically dominate their opponents, sometimes achieving their objectives withou having to do much fighting.

During their relentless advance through Burma in the first five months o 1942, and during the abortive British offensive in Arakan the following year the Japanese forced the British to play to their tune. The Japanese method o war, their single-minded determination to win, together with their savagery and wanton disregard for life – either their own or their enemy's – came as a brutal shock to the European military tradition and its deeply rooted codes of military conduct and chivalry that still held sway in the Indian and Burma Armies. To the ordinary fighting man – but particularly the Indian and British soldier (the Gurkha was not similarly affected) – the Japanese soldier quickly gained fame as a fearsome fighting beast for which none of their training had prepared them. Their ferocity in the offensive (such as the invasion of Burma in 1942) and their remarkable staying power when on the defensive (such as in Arakan in 1943) gave the Japanese a dramatic psychological advantage over Indian and British troops and allowed them to dominate the battlefield, creating an aura of invincibility about the Japanese 'superman' that was to take two years for the British to erase.

However, despite these stunning early successes, the IJA remained remarkably backward in adopting modern methods and equipment. Its supply arrangements were simplistic, its artillery provision was weak and its air support virtually non-existent. In the three months between April and June 1944 the total number of Allied air sorties including transport flights directly in support of Imphal and Kohima exceeded 30,000. In contrast, limited aircraft numbers meant that the Japanese could mount a mere 1,750 sorties over the battlefields during this time, and by the end of July only 49 aircraft remained in the Japanese inventory. A significant Japanese weakness lay in the fact that most of their aircraft were fighters: Tazoe possessed no transport capability and only a tiny bomber force that was frittered away early in the fighting. One of Tokyo's worst miscalculations in 1944 was failing to anticipate the combined strength of Allied air forces, without which the defence of India would not have been possible. Both Kawabe and Mutaguchi saw the invasion of India as an exercise in ground warfare and in their assessments (if, indeed, they ever made them) of Allied air power they failed grievously to appreciate this war-winning capability enjoyed by their enemy, and their own dramatic weakness in this regard.

The Japanese were ignorant of the improvement in British training, tactics, leadership and morale since 1942–43. They believed that it would be impossible for the British to deploy tanks so did not equip their men with proper anti-tank weapons, and they substituted (in 31st Division) heavy field artillery for lighter calibre mountain artillery. Their logistical plans were wildly optimistic. Equally, the dynamism of Japanese leadership which secured such dramatic successes in 1942 had waned significantly by 1944 and left them less able to cope with a very different battlefield and a vastly different enemy from that which they had encountered in 1942 and early 1943. Japanese generalship was, in the main, focused on retaining the loyalty of Japanese soldiers to their calling as soldiers of the emperor, and their duty to die rather than to surrender. The result was slaughter on an immense scale, as Japanese soldiers followed their commanders to earthly oblivion and (they presumed) heavenly glory.

BRITISH FORCES

Pushed out of Burma in May 1942, following a 1,600km (1,000-mile) retreat back to India, the British had been humiliated by Japanese boldness, professionalism and panache. The limited offensive into Burma along the Arakan coast in May 1943 had ended in dismal failure, demonstrating once again that at the time British and Indian troops remained ill matched against the hardy, aggressive, triumphant Japanese.

British troops wait watchfully in a well-constructed bunker in one of the Kohima battle areas. A sign of the obvious tension of the moment is that the men have not removed their steel helmets. (IWM, Ind 3486)

Indian engineers of the Madras Sappers and Miners building a log corduroy track from Kohima to the village of Jessami to the north. In the absence in the region of any other road-building materials the British had resorted before the Japanese invasion to cutting thousands of trees and laying them on the surface of tracks as a means of extending their life. It meant, however, that vehicles were forced to travel extremely slowly. (IWM, Ind 3515)

By early 1944, however, much had changed in the British/Indian Army, and the Japanese now found themselves facing an enemy that was immeasurably better prepared, equipped, trained and led than it had been only eight months before. Lieutenant-General Bill Slim was convinced that he could transform the fortunes of his troops, despite the many gainsayers who loudly claimed the Japanese to be unbeatable. His basic prescription – in which a new raft of divisional commanders such as Douglas Gracey, Ouvry Roberts and Frank Messervy among others supported him wholeheartedly – was rigorous and realistic training for all troops. Imaginative and demanding training was instituted, both at the level of the individual and that of the unit – section, platoon, company and battalion. Training in simulated battlefield conditions would enable soldiers to cope with the demands of fighting a tenacious enemy in the harsh physical environment of both mountain and jungle. He was certain that if men were adequately prepared to overcome these challenges, if they were helped to do so by better medical care (especially to prevent the mass casualties caused in 1942 and 1943 by malaria) and if the lines of communication that supplied troops in forward areas with food, fuel and ammunition were made more secure – by using air supply rather than relying on tracks and roads – morale would improve, and with it the troops' certainty that they could defeat the Japanese in battle.

Despite the demands posed by the torrential monsoon rains that fell each year between May and October physical toughening, weapons training and long cross-country marches – on foot and with mules – carried out over hills, through jungle and across rivers became the order of the day. Live firing with rifles, machine-guns and grenades in realistic conditions – often at the end of

A Naga road-building gang, 1944. The Nagas were enthusiastic allies of the British, rallied by their *gaonburas* (village leaders) under the leadership of Charles Pawsey, the Deputy Commissioner who lived on Garrison Hill throughout the siege. Nagas served not only as labourers, however, with many fighting directly against the Japanese. (IWM, Ind 3658)

exhausting marches over huge distances in day and night, and through the dank, sun-parched jungle – was practised constantly. Exercises ranged from patrol actions by sections and platoons, ambushes up to company level to battalion attacks coordinated with artillery and aircraft. In addition night training, field discipline and mock battles with live ammunition, mortars and artillery in all weathers became the norm. Training was hard and embraced every soldier in every type of unit, including men who in earlier times in the Indian Army would have been regarded as non-combatants. It was essential if, under the strain of battle, exhausted soldiers were able to conquer their fear, think clearly and shoot straight in a crisis and inspire maximum physical and mental endeavour. They needed to overcome the tremendous psychological demands entailed in fighting the Japanese, who as a matter of course ruthlessly exploited mistakes caused by either inexperience or complacency. In time, this training, together with carefully choreographed engagements with the Japanese, demonstrated to his men that the Japanese were not bogeymen, and could be beaten. Officers who did not make the grade were removed and replaced.

The Army was taught how to cooperate with its various arms and services, and with the Royal Air Force (RAF) and Indian Air Force (IAF). Signals, engineer and artillery courses blossomed, as did air-to-ground cooperation courses, infantry and tank cooperation training, parachute, air landing and glider training, and innumerable other courses and instruction dealing with everything from the provision of air-dropped supplies to the proper crossing of rivers.

The Fourteenth Army was well supported by air, especially by transport (largely provided by the Americans), which meant that Slim had the ability to move forces rapidly to where they were most needed. Troops on the ground, even small numbers who found themselves on long-range patrol, or who were cut off by Japanese encirclement, could depend on rapid and accurate air drops of essential supplies – including fuel, ammunition, food and water – when required.

ORDERS OF BATTLE

JAPANESE

Sato's 31st Division comprised three regiments, each of three battalions, totalling 20,000 men when at full strength. When beginning the advance on Kohima it is likely that the division was at about 70 per cent of its full strength. The structure of the division was as follows:

Division HQ (Lt. Gen. Sato Kotoku) with 300 all ranks, with a colonel as chief of staff
    Administrative Staff
    Quartermaster
    Medical
    Veterinary
    Ordnance
    Judicial
General Staff (75 men)
    G1 (Operations and Logistics) (each led by a lieutenant-colonel)
    G2 (Intelligence)
    G3 (Supply)
Detachments
    Ordnance (50 all ranks)
    Signals (250 all ranks)
    Veterinary (50 all ranks)
    HQ train (baggage)
    Guard unit
    MP detachment
    Medical unit (900 all ranks)
    Field hospitals (4)
    Water purifying unit (120 all ranks)

Infantry Group (Lt. Gen. Miyazaki Shigesaburo)
    HQ (100 all ranks)
    Signal unit
    Tankette company (light tanks for reconnaissance)
58th Infantry Regiment (Colonel Fukunaga) totalling 3,845 men
    HQ (175 men)
    Signals (130 men)
    Artillery (125 men)
    Anti-tank (115 men)
    3 x battalions (each with 1,100 men)
124th Infantry Regiment (Colonel Torikai) – as above
138th Infantry Regiment (Colonel Miyamoto) – as above

31st Mountain Artillery Regiment (3,400 men)
    HQ
    3 x battalions (980 men)

31st Engineer Regiment
    3 x companies (250 men)
    1 x material platoon (50 men)

31st Transport Regiment
    4 x draught companies (350 men, with a total capacity of 250 tons)
    2 x motor transport companies (150 men, with a total capacity of 150 tons)

The total armament of the division at full strength was:

Rifles	–	9,000
Light machine guns	–	382
Grenade dischargers	–	340
Heavy machine guns	–	112
20mm anti-tank guns	–	18
37 or 47mm anti-tank gun	–	22
70mm battalion gun	–	18
75mm regimental gun	–	12
75mm mountain gun	–	36

BRITISH

The major combat units at Kohima between April and June 1944 were as follows:

XXXIII CORPS (LT. GEN. MONTAGU STOPFORD)

Corps troops
Infantry
    1st Burma Regiment
    1st Chamar Regiment
    1st Assam Regiment
    The Shere Regiment (on loan from the Kingdom of Nepal)
    The Malindra Dal Regiment (on loan from the Kingdom of Nepal)
Armour
    149th Regiment Royal Armoured Corps
    Detachment, 150th Regiment, Royal Armoured Corps
    11th Cavalry (armoured cars)
    45th Cavalry (Stuart light tanks)
Artillery
    1st Medium Regiment RA
    50th Indian Light Anti-Aircraft/Anti-Tank Regiment
    24th Indian Mountain Regiment
Engineers
    429th Field Company Indian Engineers
    44th Field Park Company Indian Engineers
    10th Battalion, Indian Engineers
202nd Line of Communication Area (Maj. Gen. R. P. L. Ranking)

2nd Division (Maj. Gen. J. M. L. Grover)

Divisional troops

Infantry

    2nd Manchester Regiment (Vickers machine guns)

    2nd Reconnaissance Regiment

    143rd Special Service Company

Royal Artillery

    10th Field Regiment

    16th Field Regiment

    99th Field Regiment

    100th Light Anti-Aircraft/Anti-Tank Regiment.

Royal Engineers

    5th Field Company

    208th Field Company

    506th Field Company

    21st Field Park Company

4th Brigade (Brigs. Willie Goschen (KIA); Theobalds (KIA); Robert Scott (WIA))

    1st Royal Scots

    2nd Royal Norfolks

    1/8th Lancashire Fusiliers

    4th Field Ambulance RAMC

5th Brigade (Brig. Victor Hawkins (WIA))

    7th Worcester

    2nd Dorset

    1st Queen's Own Cameron Highlanders

    5th Field Ambulance RAMC

7th Indian Division (Maj. Gen. Frank Messervy)

Divisional infantry

    7/2nd Punjab (Reconnaissance Battalion)

    13th Frontier Force Rifles

Artillery

    136th Field Regiment Royal Artillery

    139th Field Regiment Royal Artillery

    24th Anti-Tank Regiment Royal Artillery

    25th Mountain Regiment, Indian Army

Engineers

    62nd Field Company Indian Engineers

    77th Field Company Indian Engineers

    421st Field Company Indian Engineers

33rd Indian Brigade (Brig. Loftus-Tottenham)

    1st Queen's Royal Regiment

    4/15th Punjab

    4/1st Gurkha Rifles

5th Indian Division (Maj. Gen. Harold Briggs)

161st Indian Brigade (Brig. 'Daddy' Warren) (to XXXIII Corps, 5 April)

    4th Queen's Royal West Kents

    1/1st Punjab

    4/7th Rajputs

6th Brigade (Brig. Shapland (WIA))

    1st Royal Welch Fusiliers

    1st Royal Berkshire Regiment

    2nd Durham Light Infantry

    6th Field Ambulance RAMC

23rd Long Range Penetration Brigade (Brig. Lancelot Perowne)

    12th Field Company Royal Engineers

    60th Field Regiment Royal Artillery

    2nd Duke of Wellington's Regiment

    4th Border Regiment

    1st Essex Regiment

Although not all the following air units supported Kohima directly they were part of the forces available to the Allies to counter the Japanese offensive:

EASTERN COMMAND – CALCUTTA (MAJ. GEN. GEORGE STRATEMEYER USAAF)

Troop Carrier Command – Comilla (Brig. William Old USAAF)

    31 Squadron (Dakota)

    62 Squadron (Dakota)

    99 Squadron (Wellington X)

    117 Squadron (Dakota)

    194 Squadron (Dakota)

    215 Squadron (Dakota/Wellington)

    216 Squadron (Dakota)

3rd Tactical Air Force – Comilla (Air Vice Marshal John Baldwin)

221 Group RAF – Imphal (Air Commodore S. F. Vincent)

    5 Squadron (Hurricane IIC)

    11 Squadron (Hurricane IIC)

    20 Squadron (Hurricane IID)

    28 Squadron (Hurricane IIC)

    34 Squadron (Hurricane IIC)

    42 Squadron (Hurricane IIC)

    60 Squadron (Hurricane IIC)

    81 Squadron (Spitfire VIII)

    84 Squadron (Vengeance)

    110 Squadron (Vengeance)

    113 Squadron (Hurricane IIC)

    123 Squadron (Hurricane IIC)

    136 Squadron (Spitfire VIII)

    152 Squadron (Spitfire VIII)

    176 Squadron (Beaufighter VIF)

    607 Squadron (Spitfire VIII)

    615 Squadron (Spitfire VIII)

    1 IAF Squadron (Hurricane IIB/C)

    7 IAF Squadron (Vengeance)

    9 IAF Squadron (Hurricane IIC)

The order of battle of the 1,500 men of the Kohima Garrison on 5 April 1944 was:

Infantry
1st Assam Regiment
4th Royal West Kents (446 men)
One company, 3/2nd Punjab
One company, 1st Garrison Battalion, Burma Regiment
One company, 5th Burma Regiment
Two platoons, 27/5th Mahratta Light Infantry
3rd Assam Rifles (minus detachments)
Detachments of V Force
Detachment, Shere Regiment (Nepal)

Artillery
One 25-pdr gun with crew

Engineers
Commander Royal Engineers, and staff
Garrison Engineer, Kohima, and staff

Signals
221 Line of Communication Construction Section
Detachment, Burma Signals
Detachment, IV Corps Signals
Detachment, Line of Communication Signals

Medical
80th Light Field Ambulance
Detachment, 53rd Indian General Hospital
19th Field Hygiene Section

Service Corps
46th General Purpose Transport Company
36th Cattle Conducting Company
87th Indian Field Bakery Section
622nd Indian Supply Section

Labour
1432 Company Indian Army Pioneer Corps

Miscellaneous
24th Reinforcement Camp
Administration Commander, Kohima, and staff

Kohima Ridge from the air, looking south. 1. Deputy Commissioner's bungalow. 2. Garrison (Summerhouse) Hill. 3. Kuki Piquet. 4. FSD Hill. 5. DIS Hill. 6. Jail Hill. 7. The road to Imphal. 8. Pimple. 9. Congress Hill. 10. GPT Ridge. 11. Norfolk Ridge. 12. Rifle Range. 13. Two Tree Hill. 14. Jotsoma track. On the extreme left is the Aradura Spur and top right is Mount Pulebadze (2293m). (IWM, MH 3082a)

OPPOSING PLANS

JAPANESE PLANS

Mutaguchi's evaluation of the British position in north-east India revealed that the three key strategic targets in Assam were Imphal, Kohima and Dimapur, the latter of which held stores sufficient to sustain an army on the offensive for several months. If Kohima were captured, Imphal would be cut off from the rest of India by land. From the outset Mutaguchi believed that with a good wind Dimapur, in addition to Kohima, could and should be secured. He reasoned that capturing this massive depot would be a devastating, possibly terminal blow to the British ability to defend Imphal, supply Stilwell and mount an offensive into Burma. With Dimapur captured, Bose and his INA could pour into Bengal, initiating the long-awaited anti-British uprising.

Whether or not they agreed with Mutaguchi it was abundantly clear to all Japanese observers that an advance into Imphal could succeed only if the issue of supply was resolved. By 1943 the resupply route into Rangoon by sea through the Bay of Bengal was already too dangerous because of attacks by Allied submarines, supplies having to rely on the railway being constructed by forced labour and POWs from Thailand. Mutaguchi was not ignorant of these issues. He knew, however, from personal experience in Malaya and Singapore, that taking logistical risks against the British could bring great rewards. This was because the British, who were usually immeasurably better supplied than the Japanese, frequently left behind large quantities of what the latter referred to as *Chachiru kyuyo* ('Churchill Rations') in their haste to flee the advancing Japanese. Accordingly, the capture of British supply dumps around Imphal formed a key assumption in his planning. The essence of Mutaguchi's plan was speed – *totsushin* ('swift onslaught') – for if these vast depots were not seized as a matter of priority, the whole offensive would literally run out of fuel.

From his experience of Malaya, Mutaguchi confidently assumed that the three Japanese (15th, 31st and 33rd) and one INA divisions allocated for Operation C would take no more than three weeks to fall on the British supply dumps. Without the capture of these supplies success could not be guaranteed, but it seemed increasingly inconceivable to Mutaguchi that a decisive, overwhelming attack against Imphal would not bring with it rapid and substantial rewards. At no time was he concerned that he might not capture the vast British depots needed to fuel his advance. Despite his optimism, he nevertheless made every effort to build up logistical capacity to

support the offensive, and did not rely entirely on the prospect of winning his *Chachiru kyuyo*. He asked Kawabe for 50 road-building companies and, taking a leaf from Wingate's book, 60 mule companies. These, however, were not available in Burma at the time and, despite Mutaguchi taking the unusual step of appealing directly to Tojo in Tokyo (over the head of both Kawabe in Rangoon and Terauchi in Saigon), he was forced to do without.

He also ordered his new Chief of Staff, Kunomura, to undertake studies into the feasibility of taking cattle with him on the hoof, an idea he borrowed from Genghis Khan. These experiments were not wholly satisfactory. The cattle's rate of march was very limited, those bred for beef were unused to carrying loads or travelling long distances, and in the precipitous jungle terrain they proved both difficult to corral and susceptible to falling down slopes to their death. Sato's division took with them 5,000 head of cattle, giving them the equivalent of 59 days of supply.

Mutaguchi knew that Scoones would attempt to hold Tiddim and Tamu in strength and decided, therefore, to appear to attack through these areas, while in fact reserving his most dangerous attack for a direction that the British would never expect. His plan entailed three simultaneous thrusts deep into Manipur: in the south from Tiddim, in the south-east from Tamu and the third to cut off the reinforcement route from Dimapur across the mountains at Kohima. These moves would conform to British expectations, and in so doing Mutaguchi correctly assumed that Scoones would then commit his reserves to Tiddim and the south-eastern sectors as a result. But cunningly, just as Scoones struggled to address the problems in the very two areas where he had always expected an attack to fall, Mutaguchi planned to launch his two most powerful attacks in the east and north. This would take the British by surprise, and at a time when their reserve had been allocated to other threatened areas. The 15th Division would cross the Chindwin far to the north of Tamu by raft and pontoon and advance across the mountains of the Somra Tracts to attack Imphal from the north. The division's line of advance was to take them through the village of Humine on the Burmese border and then along tracks and paths to Sangshak, before heading due west, crossing the road to Kohima and falling on Imphal from the north. Still further north, and directed against the mountaintop town of Kohima, the entire 31st Division would cross the Chindwin between Homalin and Tamanthi, heading north-west. In the southern prong of this advance, the 138th Regiment would make for Ukhrul, cutting the Imphal–Kohima road at Maram; in the middle the 58th Regiment would make for Somra and then Jessami before moving

Part of Naga Village after the battle, showing the ferocity of the fighting. This was the site of 5th Brigade's struggle for Naga Hill (Church Knoll, Hill 5120, Hunter's Hill and Gun Spur). (IWM, Ind 3709)

he final 50km (30 miles) west to Kohima; and in the far north the 124th Regiment would cover the northern flank in the Naga Hills. This triple pincer was calculated to cut Imphal from its external sources of supply and place intolerable demands on Lt. Gen. Scoones. Mutaguchi hoped that in facing multiple threats on all but the western side of the compass, Scoones would be unable to cope with the desperate and disparate calls for his limited reserves to fill the inevitable gaps that the Japanese attack would force in his defences. To be successful, Mutaguchi needed to ensure that his troops captured Imphal before the monsoon rains fell and transformed the jungle tracks his men would use into impassable quagmires. He also needed to do it quickly, as the supplies he could promise his three divisional commanders were meagre indeed. The date Mutaguchi set himself for victory at Imphal was 10 April. This would give him plenty of time to achieve victory before the Emperor's birthday on 29 April. If, in addition to Kohima, Sato could also seize Dimapur he would sever the head of the British hydra once and for all.

BRITISH PLANS

It was abundantly clear to the British by February 1944 that the Japanese were planning to mount at least a foray into Assam. What they did not know in any detail was Mutaguchi's precise intentions: for a long time it was expected never to be anything more significant than a raid. When it became apparent – from intelligence gleaned from ULTRA (top secret signals intelligence) and long-range 'Z Force' patrols inside Burma itself – that the offensive would comprise the entire Fifteenth Army, Slim assumed that the Japanese at the very least would attempt to isolate and destroy his two front-line divisions in Manipur (17th and 20th) and cut the Imphal–Dimapur road at Kohima to prevent reinforcements reaching Imphal, before striking against the strategic British base at Dimapur, perhaps as the first stage in a deeper penetration of India.

The Japanese invasion

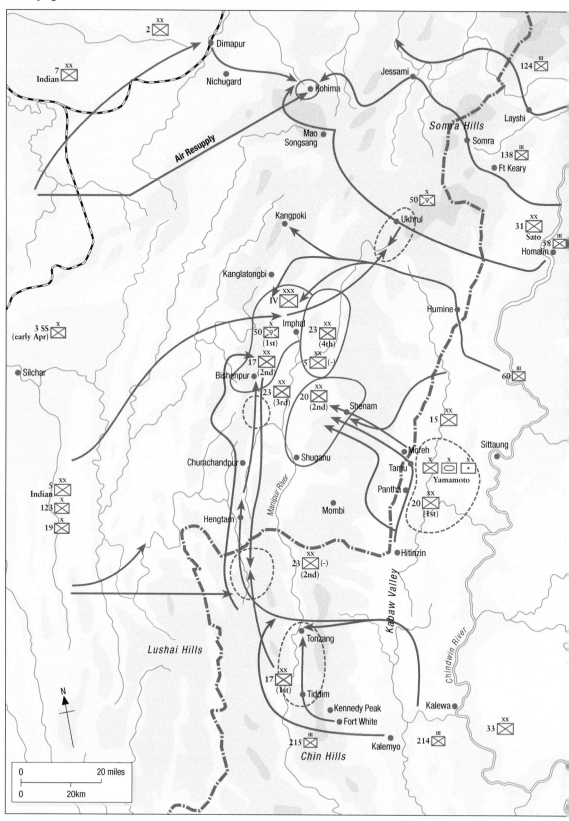

Defeating any Japanese attack was never going to be a simple proposition, as, until the demise of Operation Z in Arakan in late February 1944, the Japanese had remained unbeaten in battle against the British in south-east Asia. The plan Slim determined upon was one that he hoped would play to British strengths and exploit Japanese weaknesses. Clustered in the hills that surrounded the Imphal Plain he planned to entice Mutaguchi's Fifteenth Army into a major battle in India in circumstances favourable to the British. It was nevertheless hugely risky. The two forward divisions of IV Corps (the 17th Indian Division south of Imphal at Tiddim and the 20th Indian Division south-east at Tamu), unable by dint of geography to provide each other with mutual support, would be easy prey to Japanese encirclement and defeat if they remained in their current locations. Nor would it be possible for them to withdraw into defensive boxes in these forward locations to be sustained by air, as was the case in Arakan, because the allies simply did not possess at the time the number of aircraft required for such an enormous undertaking. Most of the transport aircraft in South East Asia Command were committed to supporting the 'Hump' airlift, the operation to supply the Chinese forces of Chiang Kai-shek over the Himalayas.

So, instead of keeping his forces forward and investing in a strong defensive barrier along the Chindwin to the east and south, Slim decided that he would instead withdraw his troops and concentrate them on the hilly outskirts of the Imphal Plain itself. The Japanese would be encouraged to advance deep into Manipur, while the two forward Indian divisions would withdraw from the forward positions they had been consolidating since late 1943. These two divisions would then occupy positions around the periphery of the Imphal Plain where, supported by the 23rd Indian Division (the corps reserve), they would hold fast against the Japanese attack. Key points, including Imphal town itself and the six airfields on the plain would be transformed into defensive bastions capable of defending themselves unaided for at least ten days. Allowing them to advance directly onto Imphal would stretch the Japanese supply lines through more than 160km (100 miles) of jungle-clad hills from the Chindwin. By contrast, IV Corps would, by withdrawing, enjoy vastly reduced lines of communication and benefit from concentration.

Looking north from old Japanese defensive positions on Jail Hill. The road snaking around the western edge of Kohima Ridge is overlooked, with Kohima Ridge to the left. The bungalow and tennis court area is in the mid ground above the road, and the left-hand edge of Naga Hill can be seen in the distance. (IWM, MH 3083)

A dramatic aerial photograph of the Kohima Ridge taken on 15 April 1944, ten days into the siege. The photo is taken looking south-east, with the IGH Spur prominent immediately below. Smoke from the fighting can be seen above Kuki Piquet. (IWM, MH 4109)

The British would then take advantage of their growing strength in aircraft, armour and artillery while simultaneously exploiting the enemy's weaknesses in logistics and resupply, problems that would be compounded by the onset of the monsoon at the end of April. It was a risky plan, because withdrawals, even for the best of intentions, are never good for morale.

One factor that worked strongly in Slim's favour was his opposite number's impetuous, emotional and egotistical character. Pulling back from their forward positions to the Imphal Plain would be precisely what Mutaguchi expected of the weak and timid British, and reinforce Japanese expectations of an early and easy victory. The Japanese assumed that the British would have no stomach for a fight and would crumble quickly under pressure. The gamble that Slim took, of course, was that his troops would not break and that once concentrated on the Imphal Plain, with a clear superiority in armour, artillery and air power, IV Corps would prove to be too hard a nut for Mutaguchi to crack. His three divisions would be closely concentrated so they could support each other if necessary. Although he fully expected Mutaguchi to cut the road from Imphal to Dimapur in the area of Kohima, Slim had another card up his sleeve to counter any lack of supply by land, one that had so dramatically helped to bring victory to Messervy's cut-off division in Arakan: air supply.

The Japanese very nearly wrong-footed both Slim and Scoones. Slim thought that no more than a regiment would be tasked with closing the road at Kohima and had no idea until the battle began to break that Sato's entire division would attempt to break through the non-existent defences at Kohima and pour down into the Brahmaputra Valley.

THE JAPANESE INVASION

Mutaguchi's northern columns began crossing the Chindwin on 15 March, Yamauchi's 15th Division crossing at Thaungdut and Sittaung and Sato's 31st Division further north at Homalin, Kawya and Tamanthi. At least 45,000 fighting troops, accompanied by many thousands of porters, made their way into the jungle-covered hills along the carefully reconnoitred paths towards Sangshak and Kohima. The 15th Division was to follow the tracks to Ukhrul, push onwards to cut the Imphal–Kohima road, and then fall on Imphal from the north. The 31st Division was to make all speed for Kohima.

Lieutenant-General Scoones discounted the idea that any substantial advance could be made by an invader through the hill country between the Chindwin and Ukhrul; its deeply tangled, jungle-covered hills rendered it unnavigable, so the British thought, to a large force. Consequently, the territory (centring on Ukhrul) had only the lightest of garrisons and no real defences. Forces in the area comprised two battalions of the newly raised and part-trained 50th Indian Parachute Brigade (comprising the Gurkha 152nd Battalion and the Indian 153rd Battalion) whose young and professional commander, 31-year-old Brigadier M. R. J. ('Tim') Hope-Thompson had persuaded the powers that be in New Delhi to allow him to complete the training of his brigade in territory close to the enemy. At the start of March the brigade HQ and one battalion had arrived in Imphal, and began the leisurely process of shaking itself out in the safety of the hills north-east of the town. To the brigade was added the 4/5th Mahrattas under Lieutenant-Colonel Trim. Sent into the jungle almost to fend for themselves, it was not expected that they would have to fight, let alone be on the receiving end of an entire Japanese divisional attack. They had little equipment, no barbed wire and little or no experience or knowledge of the territory.

In the first light of dawn on 19 March, Hope-Thompson received anxious calls from the commanders of both his 152nd Battalion and the 4/5th Mahrattas to say that they could see heavy columns of Japanese clearly marching on their undefended encampment at Sheldon's Corner, a few short kilometres to the east. These were troops of the 31st Division (2/58th and 3/58th Regiment), making their way along a British-built jeep track to Ukhrul, whence they would head north-west towards the Kohima road. General Miyazaki, the commander of the divisional infantry, commanded this particular column. Sweeping aside a forward company of the 152nd Battalion (only 24 survivors made it back from an original 170) Hope-Thompson desperately brought his dispersed forces (totalling 1,850 men) together at the deserted Naga village of Sangshak by 21 March. His brigade, when

The battle of Sangshak, 19–26 March 1944

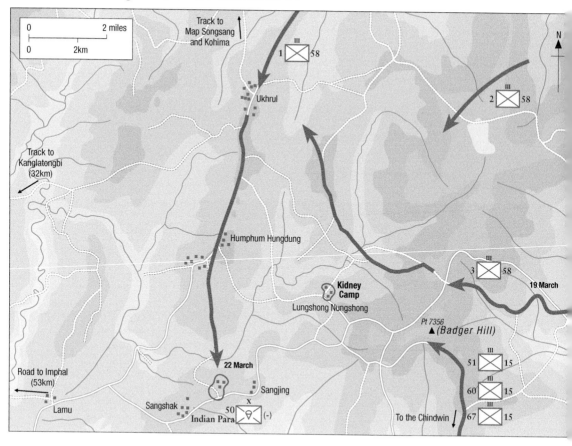

concentrated, consisted of 1,850 men. However, as the troops dug in they discovered to their discomfort that they were atop an ancient volcano, and the rock was impervious to their picks. All they could dig were shallow trenches, which provided ineffective protection from Japanese artillery. Like all Naga villages that at Sangshak was perched on a hill, and had no water; anything the men required had to be brought up from the valley floor, through the rapidly tightening Japanese encirclement.

The Japanese attacks began late on 22 March. Hoping to overwhelm the defenders the Japanese attacked immediately, throwing infantry forward into the assault without undertaking a detailed reconnaissance, or waiting for the arrival of supporting artillery. It was a serious error. The 400 waiting Gurkhas of the 153rd Battalion could not believe the sight before them as, facing north-west across the valley to West Hill in the failing light of early evening, a swarming mass of enemy rushed to overwhelm what they had imagined to be weak and puny defences. Wave after wave of enemy were cut down as they ran down the slopes of the hill into the precision fire of the 153rd's Lee-Enfields and the chattering Vickers firing above and behind them. In addition to four mountain guns Hope-Thompson's brigade also had 3in. mortars. The Japanese 8th Company of 2/58th lost 90 out of 120 men in the space of 15 minutes. They learned their lesson, however, and the defenders of Sangshak never again faced such ripe targets. Instead, as the days drew out they were subjected to increasingly frantic Japanese efforts to break into Hope-Thompson's position. Gallant attempts to drop precious water to the beleaguered troops, as well as

A rare colour photograph, taken two years before the Japanese invasion of India and the battle for Kohima. The photograph looks due west, in the direction of Dimapur. The Dzuza Valley falls away in the centre. (IWM, Col 214)

Two proud young Naga men pose for the camera in native dress, in a photograph taken in 1942. When the Japanese brought war to the Naga Hills two years later the Naga people fought determinedly and at considerable cost, for their liberation. (IWM, Col 222)

ammunition for the mortars and mountain guns, largely failed, about three-quarters of these valuable cargoes repeatedly floating down to the Japanese. Although the weight of Japanese attacks tended to be on the north and west of the perimeter facing the 152nd and 153rd Battalions, as the days went by increasingly strong probes were made against the Mahrattas on the eastern edge.

Hope-Thompson's men found themselves alone and faced by heavy odds. Unfortunately, with no barbed wire, no water and rapidly diminishing reserves of ammunition the long-term prognosis for the hugely outnumbered 50th Indian Parachute Brigade was never in doubt if Miyazaki decided to delay his advance to Kohima in order to crush the defenders.

An aerial photograph looking south-west towards Mount Pulebadze in the distance. Jail Hill can be seen on the right, with the road separating it from DIS Hill (the extreme left-hand edge of Kohima Ridge) to the right. (IWM, MH 2723)

The Japanese launched repeated and ferocious attacks on the Sangshak perimeter until on Saturday 26 March the survivors were ordered to withdraw through the Japanese encirclement. Fortunately, the Japanese were equally exhausted and did not follow up the British withdrawal. While the 50th Indian Parachute Brigade was virtually destroyed in the four days of the Sangshak battle (152nd Gurkha Battalion lost 350 men – 80 per cent of its strength – and 153rd Indian Battalion lost 35 per cent), considerable benefit fell to IV Corps by their sacrifice. The battle cost Miyazaki probably 1,000 casualties and his advance on Kohima was held up for a week, causing serious delay to Sato's plans. From both the 2/58th and 3/58th Miyazaki had lost six of his eight company commanders, as well as most of the platoon commanders. Miyazaki's speculative attack on Sangshak drew him into an unnecessary battle of attrition that delayed the journey of his column to Kohima and proved in time to be a serious setback to Mutaguchi's hopes of capturing all of his objectives within three weeks. It was the first sign on this front that Mutaguchi's plan was turning awry: the British at first seemed intent on flight, but here was stubborn – even fanatical – resistance, and it took the Japanese by surprise.

With the imminent threat to Manipur the British had been rapidly reinforcing their forces in Assam. The experienced 5th Indian Division had begun to fly into Imphal in mid-March from the battlefield in Arakan, one brigade of which – the 161st Brigade – flew into Dimapur to reinforce Kohima. In addition Slim asked for and was promised Maj. Gen. Grover's British 2nd Division (part of Lt. Gen. Montagu Stopford's XXXIII Corps, the army group reserve) should it become necessary, which Slim intended to send to Arakan to replace the 5th Indian Division. In addition Giffard agreed also to give Slim the 23rd Long Range Penetration Brigade, commanded by Brigadier Lancelot Perowne, which was still in India, in order to operate against the flank of a Japanese attack on Dimapur. Giffard also decided that once the airlift of the 5th Indian Division was complete the 7th Indian Division would then also be airlifted to Manipur. On 27 March Slim asked that Grover's 2nd Division be sent not to Arakan, but to Dimapur instead. This brought its own problems, as the earliest it could arrive was the first week of April, although the division was already on the move, travelling by train across India in the direction of Calcutta.

THE SIEGE OF KOHIMA

Because Kohima lies 193km (120 miles) beyond the Chindwin, across formidably mountainous terrain far beyond where anyone expected the Japanese might be able to reach in strength it was assumed that the most the Japanese could infiltrate was a regiment of three battalions (i.e., the equivalent of a British brigade). The ridge guards the only route between Dimapur and Imphal: if Kohima fell, Imphal would be without access to succour or supplies, and with the further prize of India beyond. In any case Lt. Gen. Slim believed that the real prize were the Japanese to penetrate this far was at Dimapur, where vast depots and stores had been assembled to support the growing forces in Manipur, together with the entire structure supporting the Chinese/American forces under Lieutenant-General 'Vinegar Joe' Stilwell in the north. What would the Japanese gain by securing Kohima if they failed to seize the British supplies in Dimapur? It made no sense to Slim for the Japanese to attack Kohima without pressing on to threaten Dimapur.

Giffard, Slim and Scoones met in Imphal on 20 March to consider the impending crisis. As yet, they did not know the true scale of the imminent threat to Kohima. This was not realized by the British until it was nearly too late. Slim claims that he had realized within a week of the start of the offensive (i.e., by 22 March) that the situation at Kohima was likely to be more dangerous than he had anticipated. It seems clear, however, that even by early April Slim had still not realized that the bulk of Sato's 31st Division was pushing on to the town. If he had known that this was the case he would undoubtedly have defended the ridge robustly to prevent its capture. The situation was grave. Far to the south the 17th Indian Division and the major part of the 23rd Indian Division, as well as the 20th Indian Division, were withdrawing in contact with the enemy to Imphal, and Hope-Thompson's unprepared and weakened 50th Parachute Brigade had suddenly and unexpectedly been confronted by the large numbers of enemy in the Ukhrul area the day before. In addition enemy forces were known to be moving on Kohima and it was assumed that the Japanese were likewise closing in on Silchar to the south-west.

Certain that Scoones now had enough on his plate with the defence of Imphal, Slim gave temporary responsibility for the defence of Dimapur and Kohima to Major-General Ranking, commander of the 202nd Line of Communication Area. Ranking was to transfer responsibility to Stopford when the latter arrived with his XXXIII Corps in early April. When fully constituted the corps was to consist of the 5th and 7th Indian Divisions and the British 2nd Division. On 22 March Slim ordered a scratch garrison

under Colonel Hugh Richards to move forward to Kohima to act as a forward defence for Dimapur. When, exactly a week later, 'Daddy' Warren's experienced 161st Brigade arrived from Arakan Slim sent it directly to Kohima to assist in the defence of the ridge. Slim told Warren that he expected the Japanese to arrive at Kohima by 3 April and to reach Dimapur by 10 April, by which time only one brigade of the 2nd Division would have arrived to support the defence of this strategically vital base area.

Stopford's plan was to concentrate his corps as it arrived at Jorhat, 105km (65 miles) north-east of Dimapur, ready to launch a counterstroke against Dimapur if in the meantime the base had been occupied or was under attack by the Japanese. One brigade would be dispatched as soon as it arrived to hold the Nichugard Pass, 13km (8 miles) south-east of Kohima on the road to Dimapur, in order to support 161st Brigade already defending the village. Finally, Perowne's 23rd LRP Brigade would be diverted to the defence of Kohima. The brigade, which was expected to arrive on 12 April, would be used to strike south on Kohima and to the east of it to disrupt and cut the Japanese line of communication back to the Chindwin.

On 29 March Sato's 31st Division cut the Imphal–Kohima road at Milestone 72. The race to feed units in to Dimapur before the arrival of the Japanese was now one of dramatic urgency. With Stopford's troops still several days away following their diversion from Chittagong, the question of how to defend Kohima and Dimapur became critical. There was no simple solution, as the sum total of experienced combat troops available before Grover's 2nd Division arrived was Warren's 161st Brigade (1/1st Punjab, 4/7th Rajputs and 4th Royal West Kents). On 29 March Slim met to discuss the issue, first in Imphal with Scoones and Stopford and then later in the day, after a short flight from Imphal, with Ranking at Dimapur. Stopford, as incoming corps commander, was concerned that if 161st Brigade was surrounded and isolated at Kohima before Grover's division arrived there would be nothing with which to defend Dimapur. Slim agreed that this was a serious risk but argued that a well-defended Kohima would certainly force Sato to deal with it prior to proceeding to Dimapur, thus giving valuable breathing space to Stopford to move the remainder of the 2nd Division into position. A compromise of sorts was reached, but as with most compromises some clarity regarding the main intention was lost.

Following these two meetings Slim issued his orders to Ranking in writing. Ranking was to prepare Dimapur for defence and hold it when attacked; to reinforce Kohima and hold it to the last; and to prepare for the reception of

LEFT
A photograph of a bunker on Garrison Hill with Kuki Piquet behind and the bunker taken by Colonel H. C. R. Rose DSO. This image demonstrates the physical effect on the landscape of the bitter fighting for possession of the ridge between 5 April and 13 May. (IWM, MH 33898)

RIGHT
A photograph taken by Lieutenant-Colonel Rex King-Clark, commanding officer of the Manchester Regiment, of Kohima Ridge, IGH and Treasury Spur. At the time the photograph was taken the fighting had moved on towards the Chindwin. Tents have sprouted over the site of the IGH Spur, and to the right, although the foliage on Kohima Ridge remains heavily denuded, the many parachutes which littered the trees during the fighting have already been gathered in by the local Nagas. (IWM, HU 44435)

Looking north-east, with the edge of the Kohima Ridge on the left, in a photograph taken on 10 May, three days before the bungalow and tennis court area finally fell to the Dorsets and a handful of Lee Grant tanks. (IWM, MH 4171)

the reinforcements from XXXIII Corps that were on their way from elsewhere in India. Ranking interpreted in these orders no instruction to evacuate 161st Brigade from Kohima. Indeed, Warren's troops, on Slim's orders, were arriving that very day after having flown directly into Dimapur from Arakan. Meanwhile Stopford concentrated on moving his Corps HQ to Jorhat, where it was established on 3 April. That night, the day before Ranking formally transferred command, Stopford made what proved to be a serious error of judgement. Still firmly of the belief that the Japanese objective was Dimapur, and in response to erroneous intelligence that Japanese units were at that very moment in the process of outflanking Kohima, Stopford ordered Ranking to withdraw 161st Brigade from Kohima immediately. All involved in the defence of Kohima – Warren, Colonel Hugh Richards and the civilian Deputy Commissioner, Charles Pawsey – were aghast at, and protested about the decision. When told that the Japanese were outflanking Kohima to the north Pawsey scoffed, retorting that if true, 'my Nagas would have told me'.

Despite this, that evening the two battalions had fallen back several miles along the road to Nichugard, leaving in Kohima a weak garrison comprising two companies of the Nepalese Shere Regiment and about 260 men of the Assam Rifles under the command of Major 'Buster' Keene, together with odds and sods recovering in the hospital and manning the depots. Ranking, sure that Stopford was making a mistake, went over the head of his new superior officer and called Slim directly by telephone to petition him to leave Warren at Kohima. Slim, perhaps unwilling to overrule Stopford, and in any case as convinced as Stopford that Dimapur was the Japanese objective, confirmed

Kohima Ridge and Naga Village

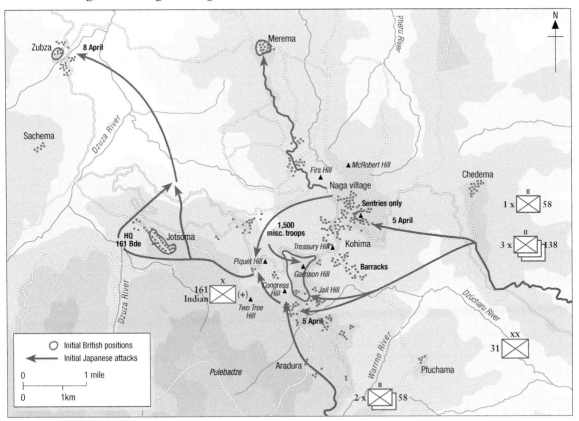

Stopford's original order. The compromise reached on 30 March had not led to a clear understanding of whether, with the limited troops available, it was better to defend Kohima or Dimapur. Warren's 161st Brigade, which had been in the process of organizing the desperately needed defence of the ridge, left Kohima virtually undefended only one day before Japanese attacks began. Had Warren's men been allowed to remain where they were the trauma of the siege that followed would have been much reduced and the stranglehold that Sato was able to maintain on the vital road to Imphal for two long months would have been significantly weaker than it turned out to be.

During this week of embarrassing confusions Sato was rapidly and skilfully pushing his columns through the mountainous terrain from the Chindwin. The only British defences in the Naga Hills comprised V Force watching posts in the mountaintop villages (a British-officered, locally recruited intelligence-gathering organization), a company of the Assam Regiment at Jessami and another at Kharasom, several days' march forward of Kohima. In the weeks before they first arrived in these villages in force, Japanese and INA reconnaissance patrols had moved extensively across the Naga Hills, identifying tracks and sources of food. There were many signs from mid-March – and even earlier in villages along the Chindwin – that Japanese troops were deep in the region.

At Jessami the young and inexperienced soldiers of the Assam Regiment had, like their compatriots at Sangshak, fought like veterans, astounding the Japanese of Colonel Torikai's 138th Regiment by the ferocity – and determination – of their response, even when they knew themselves to be surrounded by an overwhelming enemy force. When ordered to withdraw to

Kohima the youthful company commander, Captain Young, instructed his sepoys to leave, remaining at his post on the night of 31 March while his men slipped out through gaps in the perimeter until his position was swamped the next morning by men of at least one Japanese battalion, this extraordinarily brave young officer firing his Bren gun and throwing grenades to the last.

On the morning of 4 April Japanese troops from 1/58th Regiment attacked the southern edge of Kohima at GPT Ridge after a march of some 250km (160 miles) in 20 days over terrain which both Scoones and Slim had considered impassable to large bodies of troops, and following the bloody battle at Sangshak. It was a remarkable feat and in its execution Ranking and Warren's worst fears were realized, the Japanese arriving, albeit in small numbers, only hours after Warren had withdrawn his brigade from Kohima. Troops of 2/58th and 3/58th quickly fed through the hills and valleys leading into Kohima from the east. On the southern side of the Kohima area the previous night a patrol sent out by Col. Richards into the densely forested foothills of the Aradura Spur had encountered a group of Japanese soldiers digging. A quick determined rush with the bayonet quickly disposed of these interlopers, but the news that the Japanese were so close to Kohima came as a profound shock to Richards, who knew just how poorly the area was defended. When the message got back to Stopford in Dimapur the folly of the previous instructions that Warren's brigade withdraw from Kohima were suddenly apparent. In desperation 161st Brigade immediately began to retrace its steps. By the following morning – 5 April 1944 – the leading battalion of the brigade (446 men of the 4th Battalion Royal West Kents, commanded by Lieutenant-Colonel John Laverty) had managed to rejoin the Kohima garrison on the ridge that stretched from DIS Hill to the IGH as Sato launched further attacks on the ill-prepared defenders. The remainder of the brigade were unable to get in before the Japanese tentacles enclosed the garrison.

Major Tom Kenyon's A Company were positioned on top of Summerhouse Hill, B Company under Major John Winstanley on Kuki Piquet, C Company under Major P. E. M. Shaw on DIS Hill and D Company under Major Donald Easten on the IGH Spur. At this stage the close-range shelling from four

Japanese mountain guns firing from the area of Naga Village was intermittent, but sufficient to hasten the men's digging efforts. Fortunately Sato's initial attacks were weak and disparate as he was unable fully to concentrate his forces for several days. No serious attack on the frantically digging garrison took place that day, although the initial Japanese tactic of rushing the British positions was undertaken at high cost; by nightfall on 5 April the 3/58th Regiment had already suffered 110 casualties.

The fact that the British had never considered Kohima to have been a serious risk was made obvious to a horrified Warren when he had first arrived on 29 March, no systematic defence of the ridge having been prepared. Colonel Hugh Richards had been as equally shocked when, days earlier, he had been given responsibility for its defence. Consequently the motley garrison was forced to dig in and defend itself where it could – without barbed wire, because it was prohibited in the Naga Hills – hoping that even without the detailed planning for the resupply of food, water and ammunition necessary in a defensive position, they might nevertheless be able to 'muddle by'.

Unable to get the remainder of his brigade back into the confined space provided by the Kohima Ridge, Warren decided to position his two remaining battalions (1/1st Punjab and 4/7th Rajputs, together with the eight remaining guns of his mountain artillery, from Lieutenant-Colonel Humphrey Hill's 24th Indian Mountain Regiment) 3km (2 miles) to the rear on Jotsoma Ridge, one of the Pulebadze spurs, where Kohima could easily be observed and where the mountain guns could be sited to fire in support of the Kohima defenders. This was actually a stroke of luck, particularly for the artillery, as it meant that when the battle began these guns were outside the perimeter, and hence the danger area, and were able, with the help of forward observation officers on the ridge, to bring down accurate and unimpeded fire in support of the defenders. Ammunition resupply was relatively easy from Dimapur, with vehicles able to drive up the road to the gun positions at Jotsoma. Protected from Japanese attacks by the 1/1st Punjab and the 4/7th Rajputs, Hill's guns proved to be decisive instruments in the defence of Kohima.

An airdrop to men of 23rd Long Range Penetration (Chindit) Brigade over Ukhrul village. 23rd Brigade fought behind the Japanese front line, striking against their supply lines. Their contribution to the campaign was considerable, but the physical demands of operating for several months in this unforgiving terrain was enormous. (IWM, FLM 4056)

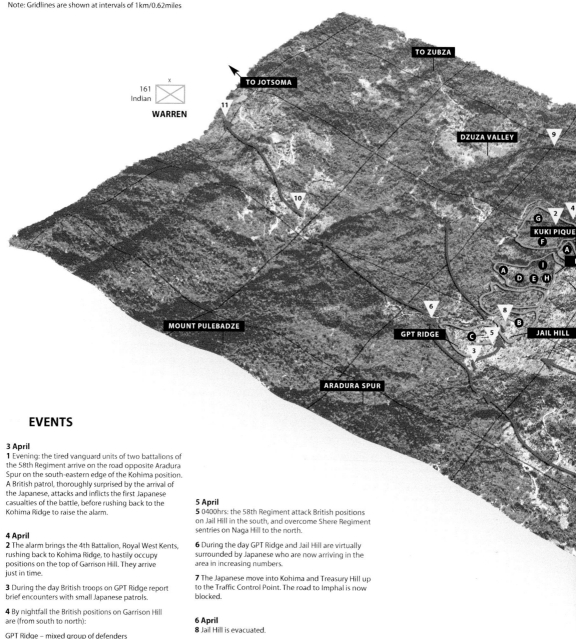

Note: Gridlines are shown at intervals of 1km/0.62miles

161 Indian ☒ x
WARREN

TO ZUBZA
TO JOTSOMA
11
DZUZA VALLEY
9
10
G 2 4
KUKI PIQUET
F
A
A I F
A D E H
6
8
B
MOUNT PULEBADZE
GPT RIDGE C 5 **JAIL HILL**
3
ARADURA SPUR

EVENTS

3 April
1 Evening: the tired vanguard units of two battalions of the 58th Regiment arrive on the road opposite Aradura Spur on the south-eastern edge of the Kohima position. A British patrol, thoroughly surprised by the arrival of the Japanese, attacks and inflicts the first Japanese casualties of the battle, before rushing back to the Kohima Ridge to raise the alarm.

4 April
2 The alarm brings the 4th Battalion, Royal West Kents, rushing back to Kohima Ridge, to hastily occupy positions on the top of Garrison Hill. They arrive just in time.

3 During the day British troops on GPT Ridge report brief encounters with small Japanese patrols.

4 By nightfall the British positions on Garrison Hill are (from south to north):

GPT Ridge – mixed group of defenders
Jail Hill – 1st Assam Regiment
DIS Hill – C Company, 4th Royal West Kents; 2 platoons 27/5th Mahratta
FSD Hill – Company of 4/7th Rajput
Kuki Piquet – B Company, 4th Royal West Kents
Garrison Hill – HQ and A Company, 4 Royal West Kents
IGH Spur – 3rd Assam Rifles
Deputy Commissioner's bungalow – Mixed group of defenders
Jotsoma – 24th Mountain Artillery Regiment; 1/1st Punjab; three companies, 4/7th Rajput

5 April
5 0400hrs: the 58th Regiment attack British positions on Jail Hill in the south, and overcome Shere Regiment sentries on Naga Hill to the north.

6 During the day GPT Ridge and Jail Hill are virtually surrounded by Japanese who are now arriving in the area in increasing numbers.

7 The Japanese move into Kohima and Treasury Hill up to the Traffic Control Point. The road to Imphal is now blocked.

6 April
8 Jail Hill is evacuated.

9 The Japanese move into the Dzuza Valley to the west of Treasury Ridge in order to complete the encirclement of Kohima.

10 The Japanese send strong patrols to Zubza, cutting behind British HQ positions at Jotsoma.

7 April
11 Japanese occupy positions at Zubza, blocking the road up into the Naga Hills from Nichugard and Dimapur.

THE JAPANESE ESTABLISH THE SIEGE 3-7 APRIL 1944

The Japanese arrival on the outskirts of Kohima Ridge and Naga Village on the late evening of 4 April and early morning of 5 April 1944 came as a profound shock to the British, who were entirely unprepared to defend this most strategic of mountain passes – the gateway to the Brahmaputra Valley and India.

JAPANESE UNITS
1. 58th Regiment (Colonel Fukunaga)
2. 138th Regiment (Colonel Torikai)
3. 124th Regiment (Colonel Miyamoto)
4. Mountain artillery regiment
5. Field gun battery
6. Field engineer battalion
7. Signals battalion
8. Field hospital
9. Transport battalion

Note: Japanese support functions were spread on the hills to the south-east of Kohima. their exact locations are unknown.

BRITISH UNITS
A. 4th Battalion, Queen's Royal West Kent Regiment (arrived on 5 April)
B. 1st Assam Regiment
C. One company, 3/2nd Punjab
D. One company, 1st Garrison Battalion, Burma Regiment
E. One company, 5th Burma Regiment
F. Two platoons, 27/5th Mahratta Light Infantry
G. 3rd Assam Rifles (minus detachments)
H. Detachments of V Force
I. One company 4/7th Rajputs
J. Detachment, Shere Regiment (Nepal)

TO MEREMA

NAGA VILLAGE

N

31 SATO

On the ridge itself the puny garrison now consisted of some 2,500 men, of whom 1,000 were non-combatants unable to make their escape along the road to Zubza and Nichugard before the Japanese net closed in on Kohima. Spread across the ridge (1,000 by 850m [1,100 by 950 yards] at most) the garrison included, in addition to the Royal West Kents, a group of disparate units that the Kents quickly but affectionately called 'the odds and sods'. These included 20th Battery (Major Dick Yeo) of the 24th Indian Mountain Regiment, a troop of Indian engineers from the 2nd Field Company, about two companies worth (260 men) of the 3rd and 4th Assam Rifles, many of whom had made their way back after fighting at Jessami, and a large number of bewildered support personnel who in peacetime had manned the various depots scattered across the hills and who had not managed to make good their escape.

Japanese pressure on the perimeter increased on the morning of 6 April; repeated attacks by Colonel Fukunaga's 58th Regiment on Jail Hill and GPT Ridge (to its rear left) overwhelmed the defenders, a mixed force of men from the 1/3rd Gurkhas and the Burma Rifles. Heavy artillery and mortar fire quickly denuded trees of their foliage, snapping branches and scattering jagged splinters to accompany the whine and hiss of exploding shrapnel. By 11 o'clock the surviving defenders were forced off Jail Hill and down into the steep valley through which ran the road, and then up into the relative safety of the trees on DIS Hill, where Maj. Shaw's C Company were desperately digging in. The Japanese attack was relentless and, although they secured Jail Hill dominating the south-eastern edge of the Kohima Ridge, they suffered extensive casualties, including Captain Nagaya, the commander of 3/58th Regiment, who was killed.

The many British casualties were crowding the IGH spur where the energetic and inspiring Lieutenant-Colonel John Young of the 75th Indian Field Ambulance was organizing an Advanced Dressing Station and tarpaulin-covered pits where surgery could be carried out. Major Donald Easten was ordered to retake Jail Hill with D Company, 4th Royal West Kents, but by

A supply train arrives at Dimapur (also known as 'Manipur Road') from the Brahmaputra River, carrying material for the British 2nd Division. The entire 2nd Division arrived in this way, after crossing the length of India, between 1 and 11 April 1944. (IWM, FLM 4066)

A mule train from 23rd LRP Brigade. These men depended for supplies on what they and their mules could carry, and on intermittent supplies dropped from the air. (IWM, FLM 4070)

now the Japanese had already dug deeply into the hillside and could not be ejected without considerable expenditure of life. Easten took his company and dug them in around FSD Hill. Since Jail Hill dominated the southern edge of the ridge defences, the disappearing tree cover became a problem for the defenders who became visible to the Japanese and consequently could move only at night. Even then it wasn't safe, as repeated night attacks and infiltration patrols, not to mention artillery and mortar fire as well as machine guns firing on fixed lines, was to demonstrate.

Despite Japanese pressure from the south (on GPT Ridge and Jail Hill) and the north (Naga Hill), welcome reinforcements on 6 April made their way inside the perimeter up the steep valley to the west. They included a company of the 4/7th Rajputs commanded by Capt. Mitchell. Six hours later the telephone cable back to Jotsoma and Warren's HQ was cut. Except for Laverty's and Yeo's radios (Richards' soon ran out of battery and he was forced to rely on Laverty) the Kohima Ridge was now cut off. Its 1,000 defenders (together with the 1,500 non-combatants milling around in confusion and impeding the defenders) squeezed inside the perimeter and were soon surrounded by up to 15,000 eager Japanese. That night, when the sun was replaced by a resplendent shining moon, a company of Japanese came down the steep slopes of Jail Hill, crossed the road and climbed up DIS Hill to a cacophony of war cries and blaring bugles. The attack was frontal, entirely without subtlety. The defenders believed the Japanese were 'psyching themselves up' into a fever of martial emotion to brave the British bullets. The fire from the waiting Royal West Kents scythed into the attackers, as did bombs from Sergeant Victor King's mortars, landing within metres of the West Kent positions.

Not disheartened by their casualties the Japanese persisted doggedly and soon, in the noisy, moonlit darkness, the situation was looking grave for the West Kents, the hand-to-hand fighting carrying on through the night, flashes of light here and there across the position denoting the points where defender and attacker fired at each other in the darkness. By the early light of the reluctant

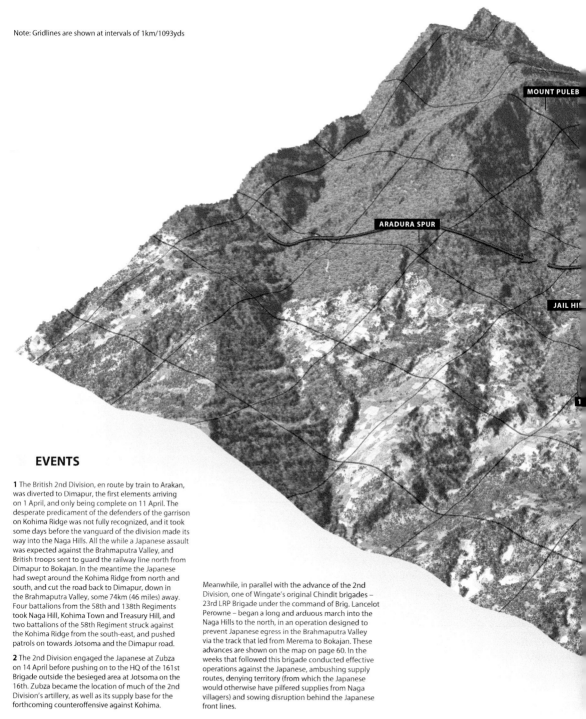

Note: Gridlines are shown at intervals of 1km/1093yds

MOUNT PULEB

ARADURA SPUR

JAIL HI

1

EVENTS

1 The British 2nd Division, en route by train to Arakan, was diverted to Dimapur, the first elements arriving on 1 April, and only being complete on 11 April. The desperate predicament of the defenders of the garrison on Kohima Ridge was not fully recognized, and it took some days before the vanguard of the division made its way into the Naga Hills. All the while a Japanese assault was expected against the Brahmaputra Valley, and British troops sent to guard the railway line north from Dimapur to Bokajan. In the meantime the Japanese had swept around the Kohima Ridge from north and south, and cut the road back to Dimapur, down in the Brahmaputra Valley, some 74km (46 miles) away. Four battalions from the 58th and 138th Regiments took Naga Hill, Kohima Town and Treasury Hill, and two battalions of the 58th Regiment struck against the Kohima Ridge from the south-east, and pushed patrols on towards Jotsoma and the Dimapur road.

2 The 2nd Division engaged the Japanese at Zubza on 14 April before pushing on to the HQ of the 161st Brigade outside the besieged area at Jotsoma on the 16th. Zubza became the location of much of the 2nd Division's artillery, as well as its supply base for the forthcoming counteroffensive against Kohima.

Meanwhile, in parallel with the advance of the 2nd Division, one of Wingate's original Chindit brigades – 23rd LRP Brigade under the command of Brig. Lancelot Perowne – began a long and arduous march into the Naga Hills to the north, in an operation designed to prevent Japanese egress in the Brahmaputra Valley via the track that led from Merema to Bokajan. These advances are shown on the map on page 60. In the weeks that followed this brigade conducted effective operations against the Japanese, ambushing supply routes, denying territory (from which the Japanese would otherwise have pilfered supplies from Naga villagers) and sowing disruption behind the Japanese front lines.

THE SIEGE OF KOHIMA

The British response to the Japanese attack was slow. The British had expected an attack of sorts against Kohima, but not until the Japanese arrived did they consider that this would comprise an entire Japanese division. Troops of the 161st Brigade – the 4th Battalion, Royal West Kents – were even withdrawn from Kohima just before the Japanese attack struck, in the belief that Sato would ignore Kohima preferring Dimapur instead. They only returned to Kohima Ridge to dig in the day after the first Japanese had arrived. Fortunately for the British, it took several days for all of Sato's men to reach the battle after their exhausting march over the mountains from the Chindwin.

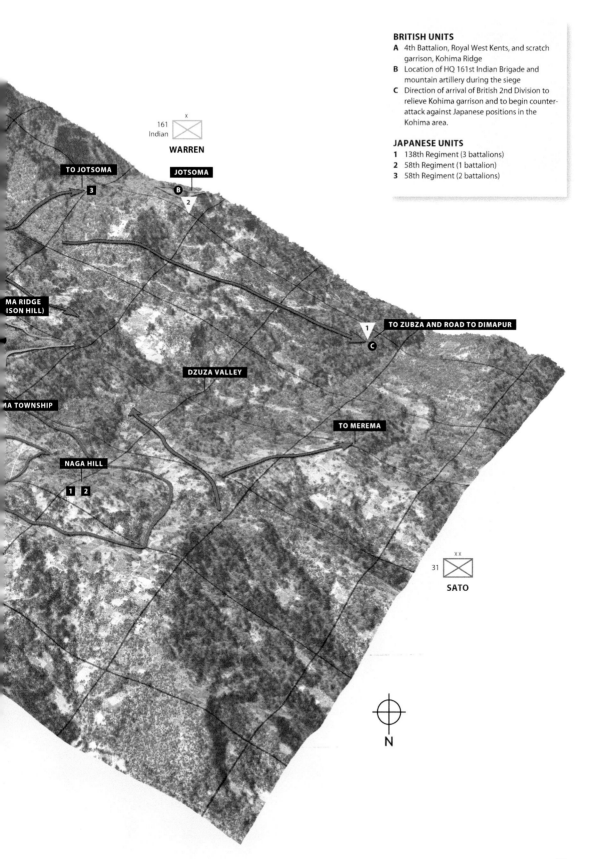

BRITISH UNITS
A 4th Battalion, Royal West Kents, and scratch garrison, Kohima Ridge
B Location of HQ 161st Indian Brigade and mountain artillery during the siege
C Direction of arrival of British 2nd Division to relieve Kohima garrison and to begin counter-attack against Japanese positions in the Kohima area.

JAPANESE UNITS
1 138th Regiment (3 battalions)
2 58th Regiment (1 battalion)
3 58th Regiment (2 battalions)

161
Indian
x
WARREN

TO JOTSOMA
3

JOTSOMA
B
2

MA RIDGE (ISON HILL)

TO ZUBZA AND ROAD TO DIMAPUR
1
C

DZUZA VALLEY

MA TOWNSHIP

TO MEREMA

NAGA HILL
1 2

31
x x
SATO

N

dawn on 7 April – Good Friday – Maj. Shaw was one of many wounded, both his legs broken by a tree burst, and ammunition was running low. When visibility had improved Donald Easten led a counterattack onto DIS Hill from neighbouring FSD Hill but, as the day flooded into light, a further menace arose: the Japanese could fire without hindrance onto the southern and south-western slopes of DIS Hill, and machine-gun fire swept across the hill, as well as the low trajectory fire from a 75mm gun, the shells of which arrived without warning. In the centre of DIS Hill a number of Japanese had inveigled themselves at the onset of dawn into a series of ammunition storage huts and the bakery, hoping to avoid detection in the daylight.

Sergeant-Major Haines led a spirited attack against these positions, dashing 37m (40 yards) up the hill with a mixed group of West Kents and Gurkhas, bayonets fixed and lobbing grenades amongst the bashas. Those Japanese who ran were cut down by waiting Bren guns; those who stayed put were burned alive as the thin structures caught fire. The bakery, whose large brick ovens in peacetime produced several thousand loaves of bread each day, was more impervious to these tactics, but combat engineers destroyed the doors with the help of large quantities of gun cotton. Instead of merely blowing in the doors the ensuing explosion destroyed the entire building, only the brick ovens inside withstanding the blast. Escaping Japanese were brought down by rifle fire. Unusually, two Japanese soldiers were taken prisoner, and although one died later of his wounds, the other provided details about the strength and dispositions of the attacking forces. Captain Shiro Sato, Nagaya's successor in charge of 3/58th Regiment, was killed. Over 60 Japanese were killed in this struggle alone, leading the men to mutter among themselves that this was a worse ordeal than Sangshak.

One of the problems now encountered by the men of C and D Companies of the Royal West Kents was the fact that hundreds of bodies lay littered across the position, some of friends but mostly of Japanese, attracting clouds of slow-moving bluebottles that feasted on the carpet of corpses covering the ground. Attempts were made to remove bodies where it was possible, but snipers and the sheer number meant that it was not possible to dispose of them all. As the days went by the effects of artillery bombardment dispersed some of the remains, with the result that DIS Hill became an unpleasant place to defend at best, and injurious to health at worst. The West Kents attempted to burn the bodies at night, but this had a poor effect on morale as the appalling smell of burning flesh drifted across the position. Where they could the Japanese cremated their dead.

For the defenders the days began to assume a monotony of intermittent terror and constant discomfort. The men knew that they were cut off from help, but they also knew that they had so far managed to withstand the swamping attacks of Sato's men. When not faced by the threat of direct attack the men crouched in their trenches, alive to the danger of the intermittent machine-gun fire that played over their heads both from Jail Hill and GPT Ridge, and from the sporadic mortar fire that would drop almost vertically from the sky with no warning.

During that night the Japanese launched both real and 'jitter' attacks against the southern perimeter, and the next morning – 8 April – it was discovered that Japanese soldiers had infiltrated back onto DIS Hill during the confusion of the night, placing soldiers and a machine gun in a bunker on the top of the hill. It was here that the fearless 29-year-old Lance-Corporal John Harman demonstrated the type of behaviour that was to lead within days to the award of a Victoria Cross, and his death. Realizing that the Japanese machine gun could cause untold damage if unchecked he crawled alone up the hill, standing up at the last minute to charge the Japanese-held bunker. Miraculously the enemy fire tore into the empty air above his head, and Harman reached the bunker door, coolly extracted the pin from a grenade, released the firing lever, counted to three (on a four-second fuse) and lobbed it inside. The occupants were killed instantly and Harman returned triumphant with the captured machine gun down the hill to the cheers of his comrades. But nothing the defenders could do seemed to slow down the relentless Japanese assaults. That night a fearsome bombardment fell on Summerhouse Hill.

By this stage, the 3/58th Regiment (fighting with two companies, the 5th and 6th) had lost most of its men and could not mount a sustained attack on its own so the regimental commander ordered the Signal Company to attack as well. On the same night that the remnants of the 3/58th attacked the southern edge of the ridge the Japanese attacked the north-east sector of the perimeter for the first time, attempting to strike through the dense rhododendron bushes 12m (40ft) above the TCP against the positions dug around the Deputy Commissioner's bungalow, and the asphalt tennis court that lay behind it, 12m (40ft) higher up the hill. This end of the ridge was terraced, with the north and eastern edges falling sharply down to the road. Gradually pressure of overwhelming numbers pushed the men of A Company, Royal West Kents, back up the hill to the tennis court where they dug in only 18m (20 yards) from the closest Japanese. In the south, and amidst heavy driving rain, the men on DIS Hill fought desperately against yet another heavy Japanese infantry attack preceded by the worst mortaring to date. Bombs landed in such profusion that several scored direct hits on trenches, destroying their occupants. As day dawned on 9 April the relief at the onset of daybreak was offset by the power exerted over the battlefield by Japanese snipers, who tied themselves to the topmost branches of trees on GPT Ridge to terrorize the slopes of DIS and FSD hills that were rapidly being denuded of their foliage, thus exposing the defenders to this new danger.

JAPANESE INFANTRY ATTACKING ACROSS THE TENNIS COURT OF THE DEPUTY COMMISSIONER'S BUNGALOW AND BEING BLOODILY REPULSED (pp. 48–49)

On the northernmost edge of the Kohima Ridge the exhausted men **(1)** of Major John Winstanley's B Company, 4th Battalion, Royal West Kents, fight to halt yet another suicidal Japanese assault across the broken asphalt of what had, only days before, been Charles Pawsey's (the British Deputy Commissioner) tennis court. It is 13 April, a day described across the besieged British garrison as the 'Black Thirteenth'. In the distance **(2)** can be seen the great bulk of Naga Hill, site of 'Kohima' or 'Naga Village' and the scene of bitter fighting in May. A British DC3 stooges off to the north-east **(3)** after dropping its load of supplies to the defenders, and a Hurribomber **(4)** of the Royal Indian Air Force prepares to come around for a bombing run over the ridge. Of the 446 men of the Royal West Kents who had begun the siege on 5 April, 150 were now dead or wounded. The men of B Company had been in these forward trenches on the tennis court since the 11th, when they had relieved the exhausted men of A Company, who had been withdrawn up the hill to Kuki Piquet. Within minutes of their arrival the Japanese attacked the newcomers, the first of three heavy assaults that night, the screaming attacks petering out in the face of almost continuous Bren-gun fire, returning showers of grenades and the accuracy of the Royal West Kent's mortars.

The Japanese now held the area to the east of the tennis court (to the right of their position as the Royal West Kents viewed it) and the Deputy Commissioner's bungalow, or what remained of it, although the Royal West Kents still held the high ground. Snipers remained a pestilence, and Winstanley's company

suffered a handful of casualties. Lieutenant Tom Hogg's platoon now numbered eight men (it should have been 30, and by the end of the siege would number only three), and guarded a corner of the tennis court. In the early hours of the morning, the Japanese tried another tactic: a silent attack, a dozen men rushing the position wearing plimsolls and carrying bayonets but this was also repulsed.

So intense was the fighting around the tennis court that no sleep was possible; men were literally 18m (20 yards) at the most from the Japanese – good grenade-throwing range – and the attacks, for the time being, were relentless. For the defenders the enemy was exhaustion, the tidal waves of fatigue that rushed in without warning to swamp men's consciousness in oblivion. But surrendering to this meant certain death. By catching precious doses of sleep, measured in minutes rather than hours, men seemed just about able to go on. Their waking hours were filled with preparing grenades, reinforcing and repairing damaged trenches, completing ablutions in the disgusting conditions and making sure that weapons were clean so they didn't malfunction when most needed. The whole position now smelt of faeces and the putrid, sickly sweet odour of bodily decay from the many hundreds of blackening corpses and body parts that lay mingled on the ground amid the shattered remains of the once-luxuriant forest. Later that night, under cover of darkness, Winstanley's much-reduced company were replaced by men of the Assam Rifles, and they crawled back through the mud to higher ground.

During the 8th, Warren's base at Jotsoma had been cut off by troops of the 138th Regiment who had crossed the deep Zubza nullah from the area of Merema to the north with the aim of cutting the road to Kohima. Sato had now managed to concentrate the bulk of his division against Kohima, and the pressure exerted by his troops was sustained and inexorable. The result was that, over the ensuing 12 days, the British positions along the Kohima Ridge would be reduced to a single hill. For over two weeks fierce hand-to-hand fighting raged, the shrinking battlefield a ghastly combination of exhausted men, mud, corpses and trees denuded of their leaves by constant shellfire. But even as the 31st Division dug its claws into Kohima, Mutaguchi reminded Sato that the real objective, the one that would make the strategic difference for Operation C, was Dimapur. Accordingly, on 8 April Mutaguchi ordered Sato to continue beyond Kohima to Dimapur. Sato obeyed, if somewhat reluctantly, sending a battalion of the 138th Regiment along the track that led from Merema to Bokajan. However, Mutaguchi's order to Sato had been copied to the Burma Area Army HQ in Rangoon and Kawabe, who had anticipated such a move by his army commander, lost no time in countermanding the instructions. Sato's battalion, five hours into its march on Dimapur, was recalled.

What might have happened if Sato had turned a Nelsonian blind eye to Kawabe's order, or if he had delayed its official receipt for another 24 hours? Sato was apparently happy to obey Kawabe and withdraw to Kohima partly because his deep-seated animosity toward Mutaguchi led him to assume the army commander's demands were motivated solely by visions of military glory. Sato's hatred of Mutaguchi blinded him to the strategic possibilities offered by continuing his offensive through to Dimapur, and lost for the Japanese a crucial opportunity for victory in 1944.

The failure to secure Dimapur while the British were reeling in confusion at the speed and scale of Mutaguchi's march on Delhi was indeed, as Slim recognized, one of the great missed opportunities of the war: it led directly to the failure of the Kohima thrust, and contributed to the collapse of Operation C. It was the consequence of Sato's lack of strategic imagination, framed by Kawabe's rejection of what he regarded as an attempt by Mutaguchi to secure for himself undying glory. What he – and Sato for that matter – failed entirely to see was that Mutaguchi was right. The capture of Dimapur might have been the decisive strategic movement of the campaign leading to a dramatic worsting of the British reminiscent of Malaya and Burma in 1942.

There was little to celebrate among the defenders of the Kohima Ridge on Easter Sunday, 9 April 1944, even if they knew (and they did not) that Sato's application of Mutaguchi's plan was strategically flawed and doomed to eventual failure. Indeed, issues of higher strategy and leadership interested them not one jot as they fought for their lives amidst the mud, blood and flyblown, blackening corpses. The numbers of wounded lying in shallow trenches around the IGH Spur where John Young had established his Advanced Dressing Station were daily increasing, the crowded area offering little protection from either the elements or incoming artillery, men being wounded for the second and sometimes third time. As the days passed the ADS became a veritable hell, men lying and dying in their own blood and excrement, over 600 wounded were crowded into in a tiny area by 20 April.

As dawn broke on DIS Hill, Donald Easten noticed that the determined Japanese had once again managed to infiltrate onto the hill and were developing an old weapon pit from where they could fire against the remainder

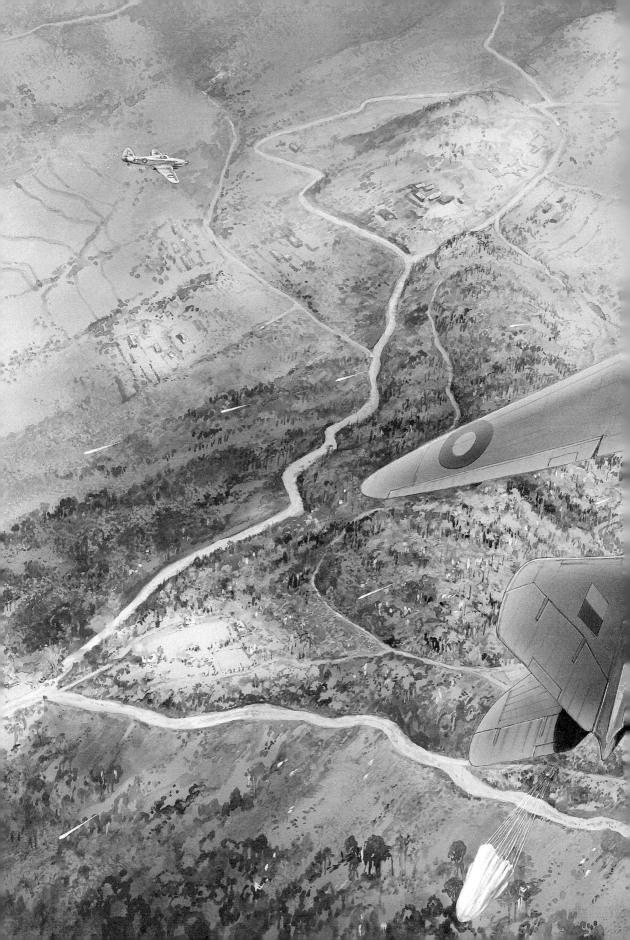

A DC-3 DAKOTA AIRDROPPING SUPPLIES AMID THE JUNGLE-CLAD HILLS AS GROUND FIRE CURLS UP TOWARDS IT (pp. 52–53)

An RAF DC3 of No. 31 Squadron on a drop of supplies over Kohima Ridge. The first drops began by No. 31 Squadron on 13 April 1944. The pilot, Flight Lieutenant A. H. 'Chick' Delaney, recalled that on his first flight over Kohima his aircraft was peppered with holes from small-arms fire. 'Our DZs were very small, and it was very difficult for the Army to leave their trenches to recover the food and ammunition which we dropped. During the next three weeks we did 15 trips to Kohima and each one was exciting as there was always plenty of ground activity.'

The DC3 has banked to allow the 'kickers' in the rear (the doors had been permanently removed) to kick out their supplies. The IGH Spur (1) is directly below, with the TCP (2) clearly shown to the left, with smoke curling up from the battle for the tennis court (3). Jail Hill (4) stands to the north of the ridge, and was the first to fall to the Japanese on 5 April. DIS Hill, where Lance-Corporal John Harman won his posthumous VC, sits opposite (5). The foothills of the vast Mount Pulebadze, which dominates the southern aspect to the entire Kohima position, sit in its dark, green overcoat (6). Hurribombers accompanied the transport aircraft in an attempt to suppress ground fire, but the Japanese ubiquitous green tracer was abundantly evident, especially during the first few weeks of the battle, the Japanese unaware that they would need carefully to manage their expenditure of ammunition until early June. They received no supplies, except for those which fell into their hands courtesy of the British themselves, which they called 'Churchill Rations'. Unfortunately, given the tiny, postage-stamp size of the dropping area, most of these failed to land on target, with precious food, water and ammunition floating down into the eager hands of the hungry Japanese. The drops did not start auspiciously. On the first day of drops on 13 April three entire plane-loads, including 3in. mortar ammunition were dropped on the enemy (which the Japanese promptly used in captured British mortars against their erstwhile owners), the men on Kohima Ridge watching miserably as the swaying parachutes floated down over the valley to the east. The Japanese and the difficult terrain combined to make each flight extremely dangerous and several aircraft, both DC3 and the cannon-firing 'Hurribomber', were lost.

of the position. Once more John Harman decided to mount a solo attack to remove this threat and, covered by two Bren guns firing from his left and his right, dashed up the hill. Frantically the Japanese returned fire but in their excitement fired wide. Harman reached the trench and, standing 4m (4 yards) to its front and firing his Lee Enfield from the hip, shot four Japanese dead, before jumping into the trench and bayoneting the fifth. He then stood up, triumphantly holding the captured enemy machine gun above his head, before throwing it to the ground. The cheers of his comrades reverberated around the hill. Harman then nonchalantly began to walk back down the slope. Unfortunately he had forgotten that with the denuded foliage he was in full view of the Japanese positions on Jail Hill. Unheeding of the shouted cries of his comrades to run, he leisurely made his way back down to his weapon pit, only to be struck by a burst of machine-gun fire in his back just as he reached safety. Donald Easten ran out into the Japanese fire, and dragged Harman into a trench. Within a few minutes, however, this extraordinarily brave man was dead.

Japanese fire continued heavily throughout the day. Corporal Trevor 'Taffy' Rees was hit and fell into a dip outside his trench. He lay paralyzed in the open, calling out in agony but unable, because of the weight of Japanese fire, to be reached by his friends. He took eight horrible hours to die, Street recalling that it was an awful way to go, their impotence in the face of Rees' despair upsetting everyone dreadfully. More men fell that day to the ubiquitous snipers. 'You couldn't do much about it' Street observed. 'You didn't know where the enemy were and just kept your head down.' The Japanese attacked again in force that night, amidst a wild rainstorm that reduced visibility to nil.

Warren was doing what he could to protect his precious guns at Jotsoma, and to help relieve the pressure on Richards and Laverty on the ridge. From his vantage point, only 3km (2 miles) away, he needed no reminding of the desperate straits in which they lay, especially as his mountain guns were pumping out shells almost endlessly. On most days the Indian Mountain gunners fired 400 rounds. But when, on 9 April, the 1/1st Punjab tried to clear Piquet Hill between Jotsoma and the ridge they encountered a number of log-covered bunkers out of which spewed automatic fire, causing 25 casualties in the day's fighting. It was clear that any attempt to break the siege by force was going to be long and difficult; it took until 15 April for these bunkers to be sufficiently subdued to allow 1/1st Punjab to occupy Piquet Hill, the final piece of ground needing to be secured before the road itself could be opened up into the garrison's perimeter.

On the ridge itself the killing continued. Large numbers of fiercely brave Japanese from the 58th Regiment were killed by the remorseless chatter of the British Bren guns, as during the night three successive assaults were made on C and D Companies of the Royal West Kents, the Japanese being denied success by the interlocking fire of eight Bren guns, whose red-hot barrels had to be changed repeatedly. Casualties on both sides were high, the Japanese attempting to gain access to the hill from the road by use of ladders, seemingly unperturbed by their losses. On the northern side of Garrison Hill the 138th Regiment again launched attacks against A Company. The attack was held, Bren guns, bayonets and grenades in the darkness bloodily halting Japanese ambitions. Victor King's mortars fired in support, the bombs landing with superb accuracy in front of Maj. Tom Kenyon's positions. It had seemed for a while that sheer weight of numbers would overwhelm the much-reduced A Company, but the reliable Brens, considerable reserves of grenades, the accuracy of King's mortars and the determined courage of the Royal West Kents denied the penetration so desperately desired by the Japanese.

The next morning, 10 April, allowed Laverty an opportunity to consider his options. Casualties had been heavy in those five nights and six days of fighting. C Company had suffered 50 per cent casualties and was ordered to abandon DIS Hill that night to withdraw onto FSD Hill through a screen provided by the 4/7th Rajputs. Supplies were destroyed and Lance-Corporal Hankinson and his section crawled to within 9m (10 yards) of the Japanese, holding their position for six hours, thus allowing C and D Companies to withdraw to FSD Hill, before crawling back all the way themselves. That night snipers continued to pick out their victims, and artillery and mortar fire continued their deadly harassment. By this stage C Company had been so reduced that on FSD Hill it was merged with D Company, and Tom Coath (who had replaced the wounded Shaw a few days before) took command. On the northern side of the hill, A Company still managed to resist the Japanese assaults over the tennis court, the strength and depth of their trenches with their overhead cover providing critical protection time and again as Japanese mortars and artillery crashed around them. The explosions kicked up dirt and dust, blinding and choking the defenders, who could never relax their vigilance with the enemy barely 18m (20 yards) distant. Showers of grenades preceded a Japanese assault, but even the fiercest and most determined of attacks always ended in failure, although each resulted in more dead and wounded among the defenders. Ammunition and grenades were dragged down the slopes each night to the exhausted occupants in the forward positions.

To cap it all, the monsoon rains had come early, and heavy, driving rain on 10 April, together with the effects of battle and of sleep deprivation, had pushed men to the edge of exhaustion. Tea was rationed to half a mug per man. Fortunately, the rain made up something for the acute lack of water within the perimeter, men lying back in their weapon pits and trenches to allow the rain to fall directly into parched, open mouths. It was found that a trickle of water was available from a pipe leading onto the road behind the ADS, behind the Japanese positions. Dangerous nightly journeys were made, through hundreds of wounded lying in the open, down the slope to the road, to fill hundreds of water bottles.

On the night of 11 April Major John Winstanley's B Company relieved the exhausted men of A Company, who were withdrawn up the hill to Kuki Piquet. Within minutes of their arrival the Japanese attacked, the first of three heavy assaults that night, the screaming attacks petering out in the face of almost continuous Bren-gun fire, returning showers of grenades and the accuracy of Victor King's mortars.

The Japanese now held the area to the east of the tennis court (to the right of their position as the Royal West Kents viewed it) and the Deputy Commissioner's bungalow, or what remained of it, although the Royal West Kents still held the high ground. Snipers remained a pestilence, and Winstanley's company suffered a handful of casualties. Lieutenant Tom Hogg's platoon now numbered eight men (it should have been 30, and by the end of the siege would number only three), and guarded a corner of the tennis court. In the early hours of the morning, the Japanese tried another tactic: a silent attack, a dozen men rushing the position wearing plimsolls and carrying bayonets, but this was also repulsed.

For the defenders, the new enemy inside the perimeter was exhaustion, the tidal waves of fatigue that rushed in without warning to swamp men's consciousness in oblivion. But surrendering to this meant certain death. By catching precious doses of sleep, measured in minutes rather than hours, men seemed just about able to go on. Their waking hours were filled with preparing grenades, reinforcing and repairing damaged trenches, completing ablutions in the disgusting conditions and making sure that weapons were clean so they didn't malfunction when most needed. The whole position now smelt of faeces and the putrid, sickly sweet odour of bodily decay from the many hundreds of blackening corpses and body parts that lay mingled on the ground amid the shattered remains of the once luxuriant forest.

The position, both on the tennis court to the north and on FSD Hill to the south, remained firm. But each day made the situation grimmer. 13 April was universally regarded as the 'Black Thirteenth'. Heavy Japanese artillery fire killed many in the ADS, including two irreplaceable doctors, adding to the misery of that bloody place. Much priceless equipment and medicines were also destroyed. Of the 446 men of the Royal West Kents who had moved back into Kohima on 5 April, 150 were now dead or wounded. The thought on everyone's minds was 'when, if ever, is all this going to stop? Are we ever going to be relieved?' Officers attempted to maintain morale, as did Charles Pawsey (he had refused to leave for the relative safety of Jotsoma), who defied the snipers each day to walk around his diminishing fiefdom, pausing to say comforting words to the bearded, black-eyed scarecrows in their trenches.

Attempts were also made to drop supplies during the siege to the defenders from ubiquitous Dakotas, although, given the tiny, postage-stamp size of the dropping area, most of these failed, with precious food, water and ammunition floating down into the eager hands of the hungry Japanese. On 13 April three entire plane-loads, including 3in. mortar ammunition were dropped on the enemy (which the Japanese promptly used in captured British mortars against their erstwhile owners), the men on Kohima Ridge watching miserably as the swaying parachutes floated down over the valley to the east. The Japanese and the difficult terrain combined to make each flight extremely dangerous and several aircraft – both DC3 and the cannon-firing 'Hurribomber' – were lost.

Desperate to squeeze the British from the ridge and to prevent them from using the supplies raining from the sky, Japanese pressure against FSD Hill remained unrelenting. Captain Mitchell of the Rajputs was killed on the morning of 12 April, and furious counterattacks against the Japanese who had infiltrated amongst C/D Company (which now comprised a mere 15 men) of the Royal West Kents failed to remove the intruders; A Company, after their short rest on Kuki, now moved to support C/D Company. That night the Japanese attempted to rush FSD Hill. The defenders were ordered to wait until they could see the whites of the Japanese eyes before opening fire. During a lull in the fighting Private Peacock from A Company dropped off, exhausted with fatigue. When he came round he discovered that he was sharing his trench with a Japanese officer who had assumed that Peacock was dead. Unable to find his rifle Peacock leapt at the officer and strangled him after a fierce struggle with his bare hands. Then, to make sure, he ran him through with the man's own sword.

Winstanley's weakened B Company were replaced on the tennis court positions during the darkness by the Assam Rifles. All the while the Japanese were attempting to get on to FSD Hill but on the night of 14 April the news zoomed around the position that a patrol of the 4/7th Rajputs had made their way up the western valley and through the encircling Japanese. Laverty told the patrol commander that although morale was high he judged that the position could be held only for a further 48 hours. Unfortunately, the message, when the patrol returned, stressed the fact that the men's spirits were high, and Warren judged that relief could wait a few more days. Colonel Hugh Richards, the Garrison Commander, issued an order of the day to the defenders on 14 April from the bunker he shared with Pawsey on Summerhouse Hill. 'By your efforts you have prevented the Japanese from attaining this objective. All attempts to overrun the garrison have been frustrated by your determination and devotion to duty…' It was a hugely important uplift to morale, but still the shells fell, and still the Japanese continued to attack. Fourteen of the West Kents were killed that day.

The Rajput patrol had the unfortunate result of raising some expectations of relief on the ridge. To the fighting men still desperately resisting every Japanese encroachment this made little difference to their lives. Instead, life and death continued their seemingly arbitrary, parallel journeys. The shattered hillside was now almost bare of foliage, the remaining trees standing forlornly, others leaning drunkenly where shells had smashed the trunk or branches. The ground was a churned morass of mud, which the defenders shared with rotting corpses, excrement and the inevitable detritus of war: scattered equipment, discarded helmets, broken weapons and unexploded shells. Yet Laverty was right; across the British positions morale remained high, despite the wet discomfort of his men's mole-like existence and the uncertainty aabout when their ordeal would end. But the troops knew that they had achieved a remarkable feat of endurance, and resistance.

The Japanese continued to press hard and on the 17th managed to force the remnants of A and C Companies right to the top of FSD Hill, the Royal West Kents then being relieved in their positions by a mixed group of soldiers from the Assam Rifles and the Assam Regiment before retiring to new positions on top of Summerhouse Hill. Above the tennis court the men of the Assam Rifles and Assam Regiment continued to defy the odds, turning back repeated attacks, but on the night of 17 April the Japanese finally took FSD Hill and successfully rushed Kuki Piquet, overcoming the sorely depleted defenders by sheer weight of numbers.

The garrison was now crammed into an area extending not much more than 320 by 320m (350 by 350 yards). But by now the dirty, scruffy, exhausted defenders could see elements of the relieving force advancing up the valley to the west through the trees below the road, and the first shells of the 2nd Division began to fall thickly on the Japanese positions guided by radio from Dick Yeo. By the following morning, the Royal West Kents on Summerhouse Hill could see the distinctive turbans of the men of 1/1st Punjab on Piquet Hill through the damp grey mist. Later that day the men of Major Ware's B Company, 1/1st Punjab, made contact with the defenders, bringing with them Lee Grant tanks that were able to make their way along the road to the side of the IGH spur, although they remained in full view of the enemy across in Naga Village.

This was not to be the sort of relief, however, occasioned by the defeat of the enemy. Rather, it was a relief-in-place, where troops from both the 2nd Division and 161st Brigade moved in under Japanese sniper and artillery fire to take over the positions eagerly given up by their erstwhile defenders. The Japanese pressed Kohima Ridge vigorously, even frantically, knowing that this was their final opportunity to seize the ridge before fresh British troops arrived, but on 19 April, the day before the first of the relieving troops made their way onto the position, Hurribombers strafed the Japanese positions, Dakotas dropped ammunition, water and food accurately on the ridge and the 25-pdrs of the 2nd Division pounded away relentlessly, firing from Zubza. The relief took place in the nick of time.

The men of the 1st Battalion, Royal Berkshire Regiment, could not believe their eyes or noses as they climbed up onto Summerhouse Hill on the morning of 20 April. Warned by anxious defenders to keep their heads down, many gagged at the repulsive smell of death and excrement that hung like a repressive fog over the position, weighing the hill down with the stench of horror. As Japanese bullets and shells continued to fall the weary veterans of the siege made their way down the gulleys adjacent to the IGH spur, strewn with Japanese corpses, to waiting trucks, guarded by the Lee Grants. The fresh relief troops on the road were astonished by what they saw when the red-eyed, unshaven survivors made their way quietly out of the trees, but were in no doubt that they were witnessing the end of the first phase of one of the grimmest struggles of the entire war, and the gallant defenders of a modern-day Rorke's Drift. 'Shabash, Royal West Kents!' called the Indian troops in warm acknowledgement of what all the defenders of the Kohima Ridge had achieved, congratulating the tired, bearded scarecrows even as shells fells among the convoy, injuring some of the wounded again and killing some, even as they were being lifted into the trucks. As the trucks crawled down the pitted road towards Jotsoma, and then Zubza, before making their slow way down through the green mountains into hot, steamy Dimapur, the exhausted survivors had long collapsed into deep, delicious sleep. Their ordeal was over.

Of the 446 Royal West Kents who had made their way onto Kohima Ridge on the morning of 5 April, only 168 remained unharmed. Two hundred and seventy-eight had been killed or wounded during the 16 days of siege in a stand which, although neither they nor the Japanese knew it at the time, would prove to be the turning point in each side's respective fortunes in the war. For the British it was also a story of extraordinary fortitude in the face of overwhelming odds. For the Japanese, driven on in desperation to overcome the last resistance before the Brahmaputra could be reached, it was an epic of dogged perseverance, a determination to overcome or to die in the attempt. Without the extraordinary stand of the garrison of the Kohima Ridge, likened without any charge of hyperbole by many contemporary observers and later commentators to that of the Spartans at Thermopylae, Kohima would undoubtedly have fallen, allowing the Japanese to flood – if they so desired – into the Brahmaputra Valley through the unguarded Naga Hills.

Nevertheless, the stabilization of the front heralded merely the beginning of the end of British difficulties. While the immediate crisis was over, Stopford now had to prevent Sato capturing Kohima and Dimapur. While the first signs of panic and chaos were now behind them, a long hard fight lay ahead for the British if they were to guarantee victory.

THE BATTLE OF KOHIMA

The 2nd Division arrived piecemeal in Dimapur, by small-gauge steam train from the Brahmaputra River, between 1 and 11 April. The entire division had rushed across the length and breadth of India on receiving their orders to move on 18 March heading, so they thought, for Chittagong. Only when on the move – on 27 March – were they told to make for Assam instead. When they first arrived Dimapur was in something of a panic, the undefended base area expecting attack at any moment and riven with rumours of the impending arrival of the Japanese.

The British reinforcement of Kohima

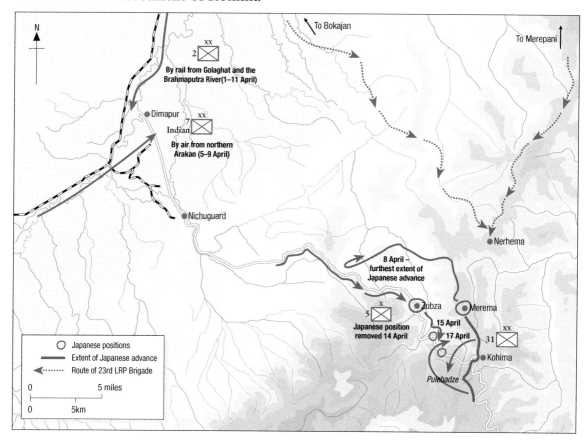

Men of an Indian Regiment, possibly the 4/15th Punjab, climb a rough track hewn into the side of Congress Hill, out of sight of the Japanese, prior to the attack on Jail Hill. Garrison Hill can be seen in the background, and Naga Hill in the far distance. (IWM, FLM 4102)

The plan at this early stage was for the 2nd Division to protect Dimapur, whilst 161st Brigade did what was necessary to defend Kohima, which, it was confidently expected, the Japanese would not reach until 6 April at the earliest. But two days later, as the 2nd Division continued to arrive into Dimapur in dribs and drabs, the panic had, if anything, increased.

The Japanese arrival in Kohima late on 4 April and during the day that followed galvanized Stopford, Grover and Ranking, all of whom were rattled by the sudden turn of events. This was the first time that most of the men of the 2nd Division had encountered the Japanese (although some of 6th Brigade had already learned of their enemy from painful experience in Arakan in 1943); they were going to learn fast. Ranking sent Warren's 161st Brigade back into Kohima from Nichugard, and the Worcesters and the Cameron Highlanders accompanied by a battery of 25-pdrs – the advance guard of 5th Brigade – prepared to move into the hills to block the road that ran the 74km (46 miles) from Kohima down into Dimapur. The remainder of 5th Brigade was warned to prepare for a minimum of a seven-day battle. As the days unfolded and Sato built up his strength at Kohima, Grover did likewise at Dimapur, although the 2nd Division was not assembled in its entirety until 11 April. By Sunday 9 April a Worcester patrol had bumped a Japanese roadblock at the village of Zubza which lay astride the Dimapur–Kohima road at Milestone 36. Two days later two companies of the Worcesters attacked this Japanese position but were repulsed in their baptism of fire. On Friday 14 April an attack by the Cameron Highlanders, following a 20-minute bombardment by 25-pdrs and two 5.5in. guns that had been found without an owner in Dimapur and 'adopted' by the division, drove the Japanese from the hill they had occupied at Milestone 37½.

Three days of subsequent fighting by men of the Cameron Highlanders and 2nd Battalion, Durham Light Infantry ('Durhams'), opened up the road all the way to Warren's HQ and the gun lines at Jotsoma. The Lee Grants fired in support of the Cameron Highlanders' last attack to clear the road, protected by the infantrymen of D Company, 2nd Battalion, Royal Norfolks ('Norfolks'). On the hill Company Sergeant-Major Tommy Cook of C Company, Cameron Highlanders (later to die on Point 5120), seized a sword from a Japanese officer

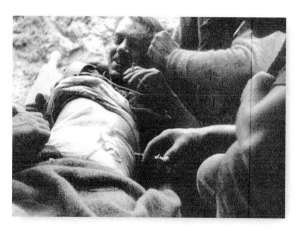

and killed its owner, along with several others. After the battle Captain H. Swinson of the 7th Worcesters walked up to watch the sappers clear the position of bodies, collecting loot as they did so. The men prized Japanese flags and the remarkably explicit pornographic postcards that many Japanese carried, incongruously alongside photos of and letters from their loved ones, the British soldiers 'bursting with laughter when they found a "filthy" one... There were soldiers' pay-books too, surprisingly like ours in character. One sapper, seeing a figure entered in red, exclaimed: "My God, the little bugger's in debt!"'

The 5th and 161st Brigades joined hands for the first time on 16 April, offering hope of imminent relief to the defenders of the parachute-garlanded Garrison Hill 3km (2 miles) further on. On Friday 14 April Maj. Gen. John Grover issued an order of the day in which he encouraged his men to 'KILL JAPS, and to KILL AS MANY of them as we damned well can' but to do so 'without unnecessary casualties to ourselves. One well-aimed bullet is all that any JAP wants'.

From the moment the men of the 2nd Division arrived in the hills they were struck by the warmth of the welcome they received from the Nagas, who saw in their arrival the first fruits of Pawsey's promise that the British would defend their ancestral hills from the depredations of the invader. The Nagas were muscular, erect, proud, clad only in short woven skirts and wearing pudding-basin haircuts. Metal-tipped spears rested in the crooks of their arms, while dull-metalled fishtail daos hung from their hips. They had a quiet, enquiring yet unhurried courtesy that belied their recent history as head-hunting warriors of fearsome potency. Their children tumbled and squealed as they played, the very young strapped tightly to their mothers' backs in the colourful shawls of their tribe, each slightly different to each other but nevertheless shot through with red, a colour that seemed more than any other to represent the Naga people as a race. The people of the hills demonstrated their support to the British in a myriad of practical ways, from portering stores to carrying out casualties, as well as fighting.

With the relief of the original garrison on Kohima Ridge, Grover now formulated a plan for the recapture of the entire Kohima area and the destruction of the 31st Division, which held positions in a horseshoe shape, each side of which faced the British advance and the right side of which rested on the Merema Ridge. His idea was that, whilst holding Zubza and Periphema to the rear, Brigadier John Shapland's 6th Brigade (1st Battalion, Royal Welch Fusiliers – 'Welch Fusiliers' – 1st Battalion, Royal Berkshire – 'Berkshires' – and the Durhams) would attack the Japanese in the centre, and gradually push

them back on the southern and south-western flanks of the Kohima Ridge. At the same time he planned two simultaneous flanking movements, one to the left (north) by Brigadier Victor Hawkin's 5th Brigade and one to the right (south) by Brigadier Willie Goschen's 4th Brigade. To the north he planned to roll up the long arm that Sato had thrown out along the valley side that ran from Naga Village along the ridge to Merema. To his right he planned something even more dramatic, namely to come at the Japanese far behind the mountain range that towers over Kohima's southern flank.

It was immediately clear to Grover, when he first saw the terrain at Zubza, looking up the valley to the dramatic ridge 'stopping the bottle' on the distant horizon, that he faced the prospect of fighting many simultaneous, small-scale, infantry-dominated battles across a wide area. The heavily jungled Naga Hills swallowed large numbers of soldiers without trace, and single sections deeply dug into carefully camouflaged bunkers could hold off companies for days; platoons could resist battalions and company positions were well-nigh impregnable without many days and nights of direct and coordinated attack from the ground, by artillery and from the air, as well as by the deliberate starvation of the defenders through encirclement. The struggle for Kohima, which was now to consume his division for the next 47 days, was not a single set-piece engagement, but a desperate close-quarter infantry and artillery battle against tough and determined Japanese soldiers holding no ambition other than to die for their Emperor, and to trade their lives for the highest price. Sato's division, when it moved from the attack to defence, dug itself deeply into many hundreds of small but interlocking defensive positions hidden in the jungle undergrowth across the entire Kohima area. It would be extremely difficult to dislodge them. To cap it off, the monsoon had also begun. The rain belted down in buckets for long stretches of both day and night, turning roads and tracks into quagmires, filling trenches and bringing with it weeks of wet discomfort. The only saving grace of the monsoon was the low rain-laden clouds that clung to the hillsides like damp blankets and which gave a modicum of protection, for periods of time, from the omnipresent Japanese sniper.

On the left flank of the 2nd Division, Brig. Hawkins dispatched the first element of his brigade – a company of the Worcesters, with Naga guides – across the deep Zubza nullah to the Merema Ridge on the evening of 18 April, to cut the Kohima–Merema–Bokajan road. The journey entailed several hours of hard physical exertion but was successful. In the following days the remainder of 5th Brigade made the journey across the valley, in single file and cutting across the front of the Japanese positions on Kohima Ridge.

LEFT
Resting British troops grab some food, probably in a village just short of Naga Hill. The helmets never come off. The soldier on the right is leaning against a large drum made of bamboo matting and used by the Nagas to store their rice harvest. (IWM, FLM 4092)

RIGHT
Indian soldiers, possibly of the 4/15th Punjab, firing their 3in. mortars from Jotsoma in support of their comrades fighting for Jail Hill. Mortars were ideal weapons in the hills, and the Japanese, when they had the ammunition, handled them expertly. (IWM, FLM 4104)

TOP LEFT
Naga warriors played a significant role in supporting the British, not just in ferrying supplies and carrying wounded, but also in patrolling and, occasionally, reverting to head-hunting practices of the not-so-distant past. (IWM, MWY23/2)

TOP RIGHT
Parachutes in trees above British bunkers on the eastern edge of Garrison Hill. During the siege (5–22 April) parachutes were the only means by which the defenders could be supplied. Unfortunately, a large proportion of these supplies fell to the Japanese, who called them 'Churchill rations'. (IWM, MWY23/5)

RIGHT
A British soldier squatting on the eastern edge of Garrison Hill, with Naga Hill visible in the background and Treasury Hill in the middle ground. The fighting on Naga Hill was to continue for a further two weeks. (IWM, MWY23/6)

Not a man was lost. Within minutes of arriving at the road on the morning of 21 April, Lieutenant Arthur Carbonell of the Cameron Highlanders, later to die of wounds sustained on Naga Hill, encountered a Japanese sergeant-major riding in the direction of Merema on a bicycle. The man was shot, his satchel revealing the orders to 1/138th Regiment to make its way to the south of Kohima and from there to assist Yamauchi's struggling 15th Division in the capture of Imphal. These orders had been received from Mutaguchi three days before. With the increasing pressure being placed on him by the arrival of the 2nd Division, however, Sato saw no way of acceding to this demand. Although he assembled three battalions on the Aradura Spur in preparation for a move south, Sato made no other move to obey Mutaguchi's order, as it would, in his judgement, have dangerously reduced his own ability to secure a decisive advantage at Kohima.

Relations between the two men, never good, were now disintegrating. Believing that he had been promised that at least 250 tons of resupplies would arrive by 8 April Sato testily demanded food and ammunition. In fact, very few supplies ever reached the 31st Division from Burma, the men having to survive on what they had brought with them, what they could beg or steal from Naga villages, or what 'Churchill Rations' they could capture from British stockpiles. Sato's fury at the lack of promised supplies reaching Kohima was fuelled by his belief that the 31st Division was being let down by Mutaguchi's abject failure to break into Imphal. In response to Mutaguchi's demand that he send troops to assist in the Imphal battle, on 20 April Sato sent the first of a number of increasingly tetchy signals to the army commander: 'We captured Kohima in three weeks as promised. How about Imphal?' Mutaguchi replied: 'Probable date for capture of Imphal April 29 [i.e., the Emperor's birthday].' Sato plainly did not believe him. On 30 April Sato signalled again: '31st Division at the limit of its endurance. When are you going to destroy Imphal?' He received no reply.

With no knowledge of Sato's developing difficulties, by 27 April the entirety of Hawkins' 5th Brigade was safely ensconced on the Merema Ridge, threatening the right flank of Sato's horseshoe.

THE BATTLE TO HOLD THE KOHIMA RIDGE

Meanwhile, in the centre the long struggle for the Kohima Ridge showed no let-up with the relief of the original garrison of the siege. The Berkshires, Dorsets and Durhams occupied Garrison Hill, the Berkshires and Dorsets overlooking the tennis court and the Durhams facing south out to Kuki Piquet. They were immediately engaged. Major Francis Boshell, who commanded B Company of the Berkshires, recalled waves of attacks every night: 'On the worst night they started at 1900 hours and the last attack came in at 0400 hours the following morning. They came in waves: it was like a pigeon shoot. Most nights they overran part of the battalion position, so we had to mount counter-attacks.' The relief of the Royal West Kents between 18 and 20 April meant that Sato now recognized that it would be better to go onto the defensive, forcing the British to attack, rather than continuing to waste increasingly scarce men on the British position that had now held out for nearly three weeks and which, despite its fragility, showed no signs of falling. One last attack on Garrison Hill was launched on the night of 23 April. It coincided with plans for the Durhams to launch their own attack on Kuki Piquet early the following morning. Corporal Bob Blenkinsop of the Durhams recalled that at dawn:

BELOW LEFT
Japanese dead in the area of the IGH. Determined and ferocious fighters, few Japanese were captured alive. (IWM, MWY23/7)

BELOW RIGHT
25-pdrs of the British 2nd Division firing from Zubza in support of the troops fighting on both Kohima Ridge, Pulebadze and Naga Hill. Zubza became the divisional support area during the battle. It was first cleared of a forward Japanese outpost by the Cameron Highlanders on 14 April. (IWM, MWY23/10)

ABOVE LEFT
Crouching British infantry creep forward before an attack on Garrison Hill during the second week of May 1944.
(IWM, MWY23/12)

ABOVE RIGHT
Unidentified British infantry, possibly of the Queen's Regiment, moving around Garrison Hill ready for attack on Jail Hill in the second week of May 1944. The Queen's and C Company, 4/1st Gurkha Rifles, successfully secured Jail Hill in fierce fighting on 11 May.
(IWM, MWY23/13)

BOTTOM
Lightly wounded British soldiers lie awaiting battlefield first aid. The man in the centre is being bandaged. Another (foreground) awaits treatment. At the time this photograph was taken the tennis court was about to fall, and the final attacks made to retake Kuki Piquet, DIS and Jail hills.
(IWM, MWY23/15)

We rushed to meet them coming forward. The battle was very intense and very bloody. I found myself in the middle of hand-to-hand fighting with a Japanese soldier. I knew if I did not kill him, he would kill me without another thought so my survival instinct came to the front and I plunged my bayonet into the Japanese soldier and moved on to the next. There were a lot wounded but we could not help them as we had to keep fighting. This lasted until the sun started to shine at the first glimpse of dawn.

The attacking Japanese were illuminated by fires, and shot down en masse. But British casualties were also heavy, the Durhams losing 15 officers and over 100 men. The discordant noise of desperate battle was incessant, a constant bass orchestra of artillery and mortars reverberating around the valley, the sounds of the weapons firing at Zubza and Jotsoma mixing with the reports of the explosions on the Kohima Ridge. The British 25-pdr gun/howitzer was an ideal weapon in this terrain, as it boasted a high elevation of fire that meant it could engage targets relatively close by. There was plenty of ammunition available at this stage of the battle, although later battles were startlingly deficient of fire support as supplies ran low. The belting staccato of machine guns added a different tone to the cacophony, as did the almost constant sound of aircraft – British ground attack and transport aircraft and Japanese fighters making forays from across the Chindwin.

The bitter battles on Kohima Ridge continued inconclusively for the following two weeks. Increasingly desperate attacks on the extreme northern edge of the ridge – around the tennis court – took place in late April to open up the road that led left from the TCP, to allow access for a troop of Lee Grant tanks to lumber up the back (i.e., western) end of Naga Hill in order to provide armoured support for 5th Brigade as it advanced slowly along the left flank from Merema. On Garrison Hill the Dorsets and the Berkshires fought to defend their waterlogged trenches from repeated Japanese assaults and the regular exchanges of grenades across the few metres that separated both sides. The plan to get tanks onto the back of Naga Hill by driving through the Japanese positions overlooking the TCP finally succeeded on 27 April, the Lee Grants trundling along the track, wary of mines, but taking the Japanese entirely by surprise at this stroke of legerdemain. Peppered on all sides futilely by bullets, they joined 5th Brigade on Naga Hill, albeit at the cost of 28 Dorset dead, who had kept intense pressure on the TCP end of the Kohima Ridge to distract the Japanese during the operation.

ABOVE LEFT
A British soldier is evacuated by fireman's lift from Garrison Hill. The men were under sporadic Japanese fire at the time, the event captured in a remarkable piece of combat cinematography by the BBC journalist Richard Sharp. The film (coded MWY) is held by the Imperial War Museum. (IWM, MWY23/16)

ABOVE RIGHT
A Japanese bunker explodes on the northern (Japanese-held) edge of the tennis court in a process of bunker clearance undertaken by men of the Dorsetshire Regiment on 10–12 May 1944. Few Japanese surrendered. Most had to be killed in their bunkers one by one. (IWM, MWY23/17)

LEFT
The process of bunker clearance across Garrison Hill after 10 May became almost leisurely. Soldiers would stand guard at entrances to kill any Japanese who attempted to escape, while colleagues placed explosive charges on poles (known therefore as 'pole charges') into the bunkers, destroying them and their occupants. In this photograph a soldier fires a burst from his Sten gun into a Japanese bunker. (IWM, MWY23/18)

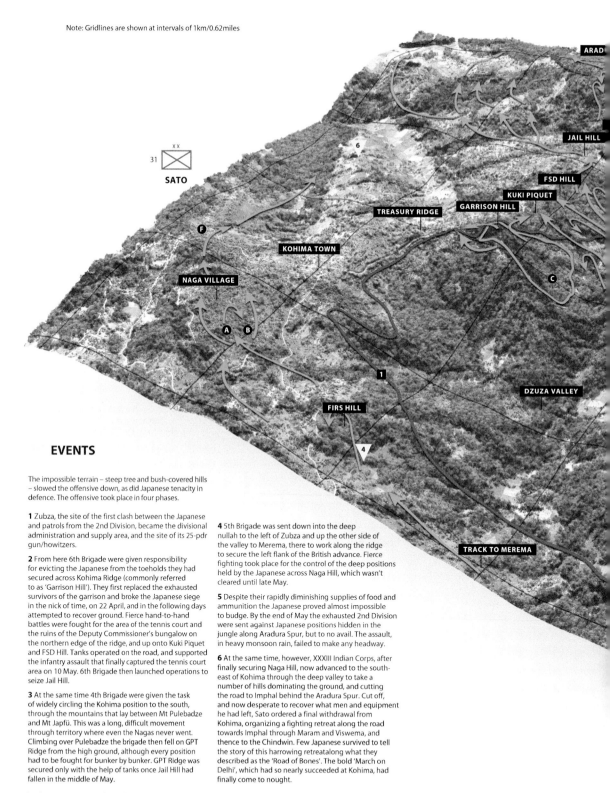

Note: Gridlines are shown at intervals of 1km/0.62miles

ARAD

JAIL HILL

FSD HILL

KUKI PIQUET

GARRISON HILL

TREASURY RIDGE

6

SATO

31

F

KOHIMA TOWN

NAGA VILLAGE

C

A B

1

DZUZA VALLEY

FIRS HILL

4

TRACK TO MEREMA

EVENTS

The impossible terrain – steep tree and bush-covered hills – slowed the offensive down, as did Japanese tenacity in defence. The offensive took place in four phases.

1 Zubza, the site of the first clash between the Japanese and patrols from the 2nd Division, became the divisional administration and supply area, and the site of its 25-pdr gun/howitzers.

2 From here 6th Brigade were given responsibility for evicting the Japanese from the toeholds they had secured across Kohima Ridge (commonly referred to as 'Garrison Hill'). They first replaced the exhausted survivors of the garrison and broke the Japanese siege in the nick of time, on 22 April, and in the following days attempted to recover ground. Fierce hand-to-hand battles were fought for the area of the tennis court and the ruins of the Deputy Commissioner's bungalow on the northern edge of the ridge, and up onto Kuki Piquet and FSD Hill. Tanks operated on the road, and supported the infantry assault that finally captured the tennis court area on 10 May. 6th Brigade then launched operations to seize Jail Hill.

3 At the same time 4th Brigade were given the task of widely circling the Kohima position to the south, through the mountains that lay between Mt Pulebadze and Mt Japfü. This was a long, difficult movement through territory where even the Nagas never went. Climbing over Pulebadze the brigade then fell on GPT Ridge from the high ground, although every position had to be fought for bunker by bunker. GPT Ridge was secured only with the help of tanks once Jail Hill had fallen in the middle of May.

4 5th Brigade was sent down into the deep nullah to the left of Zubza and up the other side of the valley to Merema, there to work along the ridge to secure the left flank of the British advance. Fierce fighting took place for the control of the deep positions held by the Japanese across Naga Hill, which wasn't cleared until late May.

5 Despite their rapidly diminishing supplies of food and ammunition the Japanese proved almost impossible to budge. By the end of May the exhausted 2nd Division were sent against Japanese positions hidden in the jungle along Aradura Spur, but to no avail. The assault, in heavy monsoon rain, failed to make any headway.

6 At the same time, however, XXXIII Indian Corps, after finally securing Naga Hill, now advanced to the south-east of Kohima through the deep valley to take a number of hills dominating the ground, and cutting the road to Imphal behind the Aradura Spur. Cut off, and now desperate to recover what men and equipment he had left, Sato ordered a final withdrawal from Kohima, organizing a fighting retreat along the road towards Imphal through Maram and Viswema, and thence to the Chindwin. Few Japanese survived to tell the story of this harrowing retreat along what they described as the 'Road of Bones'. The bold 'March on Delhi', which had so nearly succeeded at Kohima, had finally come to nought.

THE BRITISH COUNTEROFFENSIVE, APRIL–JUNE 1944

The counteroffensive by the 2nd British Division and, latterly, XXXIII Indian Corps, took place over the period between mid-April and early June.

MOUNT PULEBADZE

JOTSOMA

ROAD TO ZUBZA

BRITISH UNITS

A First attacks made by 5th Brigade, British 2nd Division

B Subsequent attacks from mid-May were undertaken by units of XXXIII Corps (Lt. Gen. Montagu Stopford) particularly the 7th Indian Division and 161st Brigade of the 5th Indian Division.

C Attacks on the centre of the position, the Kohima Ridge, were mounted by troops of the 6th Brigade, British 2nd Division.

D The task of outflanking the Japanese on Kohima Ridge fell to units of 4th Brigade, British 2nd Division.

E In late May, the final attacks on Aradura Spur took place by the combined brigades of the British 2nd Division, whilst the 7th Indian Division fought for, and finally cleared, Naga Hill and the promontories that run from it down into the eastern valley.

F With Naga Hill clear, units of XXXIII Corps swept south-east behind Kohima to join with the 2nd Division by clearing a series of hills dominating the Imphal road. Even though the Japanese had held up the assaults against the Aradura Spur positions, these threatening flanking moves persuaded General Sato to begin his withdrawal on 3 June.

JAPANESE POSITIONS

1 The red line denotes the general area of the Japanese positions, although they did not hold a continuous line. Rather, key features, such as Kohima Ridge and Naga Hill were held in strength and depth with aggressive patrolling taking place between the gaps.

2 $\boxed{\times\times}$ **GROVER**

XXXIII $\boxed{\times\times\times}$ **STOPFORD**

N

In the fighting for control of the tennis court no means of overcoming Japanese bunkers could be discovered using infantry alone, and attempts were made to bulldoze a path up to the remains of the Deputy Commissioner's bungalow to allow a Lee Grant tank to move onto the tennis court and engage the bunkers directly with its 75mm gun. Unhappily the first effort failed when the Lee Grant went into reverse, pulling the bulldozer to which it was attached back down the steep slope in a heap of crashing, twisted metal. Four days later a similar attempt with a Stuart Light tank of the 45th Indian Light Cavalry also failed, as the Japanese had brought up a 3.7in. anti-tank gun that put the tank out of action, fortunately with no loss to the crew.

TOP
As part of the clearing-up process, a British officer, possibly from the Dorsetshire Regiment, fires his .38in. Webley revolver into the remains of Japanese positions on Garrison Hill. (IWM, MWY23/19)

BOTTOM
A photo demonstrating the effect of an exploding pole charge on a Japanese bunker. (IWM, MWY23/20)

THE PULEBADZE FLANK

While Hawkins' 5th Brigade was moving into the left flank and Shapland's 6th Brigade was battling away on the parachute-shrouded Kohima Ridge, on the right flank, Brig. Willie Goschen's 4th Brigade, consisting of the 1st Battalion, Royal Scots ('Royal Scots'), and the Norfolks had been ordered to carry out a daring flank march to the south of Kohima to cut the Imphal Road below the Aradura Spur, beginning on the night of 25 April. This was a distance of 11km (7 miles) on the map, three or four times that on the ground, and it was estimated that it would take four days. It was a journey that even Pawsey's Nagas insisted was, if not impossible, then certainly not one that they or their forefathers had ever undertaken. They would give it a try, nevertheless, if the British believed it necessary. The terrain is the most intimidating and hostile of the entire region, comprising deep, almost vertical jungle-covered gullies falling between the rear of Mount Pulebadze and the face of Mount Japfü, underneath a canopy of green through which the sun

never penetrates. The third battalion in the brigade, the 1/8th Lancashire Fusiliers ('Lancashire Fusiliers'), was on loan to 5th Brigade on the division's left flank, so 4th Brigade had been reinforced by the 143rd Special Service Company, originally formed for amphibious operations in the Arakan, and stronger than a normal company, together with A Company of the 2nd Battalion, Manchester Regiment ('Manchesters'), the divisional machine-gun battalion. Sergeant Bert 'Winkle' Fitt, who commanded 9 Platoon, B Company, of the Norfolks, spoke for everyone else at the start of the brigade's extraordinary journey when he remarked: 'We didn't expect the climb and the march to be quite as fierce as it was'.

On day three, after covering 6km (4 miles) on the map, the brigade lay deep in the valley between Pulebadze and Mount Japfü, a miserable, wet and gloomy world hidden under the jungle canopy lit only by the glowing phosphorescence

of rotting vegetation, when a message arrived from Stopford. Instead of attempting to carry on to the Aradura Spur the brigade was ordered to climb left over the Pulebadze Ridge and come down on the Kohima side to fall against the Japanese positions on the GPT Ridge, which were proving a serious hindrance to the troops of 6th Brigade attempting to overcome the defiant Japanese defenders on the Kohima Ridge. The brigade accordingly turned left, climbing up and over the Pulebadze Ridge and beginning the slow descent through the jungle down onto the Kohima side. A prominent pimple above the GPT Ridge known as Oaks Hill, sitting at 1,800m (6,000ft), was occupied by the Norfolks and the 143rd Company on 1 May, the presence of British troops 450m (1,500ft) above the Japanese positions becoming known to them for the first time.

The heavy jungle on the slopes of Mount Pulebadze made it almost impossible to tell where one was, however, and judging where the Japanese position might be on GPT Ridge could not be considered an exact science. 4th Brigade had to make its uncertain way down the slopes, therefore, feeling its way, in torrential rain, alert for the Japanese. The Royal Scots stopped and occupied Oaks Hill, the brigade artillery back in Jotsoma on standby to pound any Japanese positions the Norfolks, who were pressing on down the ridge, encountered. The Japanese, alert now to the dangerous presence of enemy troops above them, moved up against Oaks Hill and fought hard to expel the Royal Scots during that first night, with no success. The morning that followed a night of screaming, fear-inducing attacks found the jungle undergrowth littered with Japanese bodies. It was usual practice for the Japanese to take away their dead and wounded, but on this occasion there were too few Japanese survivors for the task.

On 4 May the Norfolks found themselves in a position to assault the topmost slopes of GPT Ridge, led by their dynamic CO, Lieutenant-Colonel Robert Scott. Despite the fighting the previous night at Oaks Hill above them, the Norfolks achieved almost complete surprise during their aggressive and fast-moving attack. But the Norfolks managed to seize only the topmost bunkers. They had secured the upper part of GPT Ridge while, simultaneously, Indian troops of 161st Indian Brigade captured the area south-east of Two Tree Hill, offering the possibility of linking Jotsoma with 4th Brigade on the forward slopes of Pulebadze for the first time. But the Japanese bunker complex on GPT Ridge was much more substantial than the British had expected, with literally dozens of small, carefully sited bunkers littering the entire area with interlocking arcs of fire, while the entire position was also covered by Japanese machine guns further to the east on the Aradura Spur. No sooner would one be discovered and attacked, than another would open up against the attackers from somewhere else. Until the entirety of GPT Ridge was cleared, Goschen's brigade could not enjoy the short cut through to Jotsoma via Two Tree Hill; the road to Imphal remained in Japanese hands and their machine guns continued to spray fire on 6th Brigade's exposed right flank.

The other operations by the 2nd Division on 4/5 May were less successful, however. In the centre, attacks by 6th Brigade on Kuki Piquet and FSD Hill did not meet with any material success. Fighting went on throughout the day and the attacking troops suffered heavy casualties. In their attack on Kuki Piquet the Welch lost two company commanders, three platoon commanders and some 60 killed. The Durhams, whose task had been to drive round the ridge on Bren carriers (supported by Lee Grant tanks) and to attack from the western edge of the ridge, also lost heavily, although by the evening of Thursday 4 May they had obtained a precarious toehold on FSD Hill, which was to hold firm for a further week.

Catching in their eyes something of the tension of the fighting, these two British soldiers stare out from their bunker towards enemy positions on Naga Hill in mid-May. They are armed with Sten guns. (IWM, MGH88/10)

TOP
A British sentry – possibly from the 7th Worcesters – stands alert on Naga Hill. A pile of hand grenades sits on the parapet ready for use. (IWM, MGH88/12)

BOTTOM
In this remarkable photograph taken from Naga Hill, British shells can be seen falling on the base of Jail Hill, due south of Naga Hill and on the southernmost edge of the Kohima Ridge. This would date the photograph to 11 May, when the Queen's Regiment finally took Jail Hill from the Japanese. The road to Imphal, running around the eastern edge of Kohima ridge, is clearly seen to the right. (IWM, MGH88/13

THE NAGA HILL FLANK

On the left flank 5th Brigade made slow but painful progress, the Cameron Highlanders and Lancashire Fusiliers securing a small part of Naga Village during the night of 4 May after discarding their heavy hobnailed boots for quieter gym shoes, which allowed them successfully to bypass enemy positions on Merema Ridge and seize Church Knoll and Hunter Hill. Attempts at the end of April by the Lancashire Fusiliers to capture Japanese fortified positions along the ridge from Merema had ended in failure, and Hawkins decided that it would be best to bypass them, allowing them to wither on the vine while he concentrated his efforts on the main Japanese position, and Sato's HQ, on Naga Village. Unfortunately the Cameron Highlanders did not have time to consolidate their success by digging in, and heavy Japanese mortar fire at daylight forced the Jocks back to the western

BRITISH TROOPS ASSAULTING JAPANESE BUNKERS WITH POLE CHARGES AND A LEE TANK GIVING FIRE SUPPORT (pp. 76–77)

In one of the final actions that brought to an end the long and bitter struggle for Kohima Ridge and its immediate environs on GPT Ridge men of the Royal Scots, part of the British 2nd Division's 4th Brigade, storm Japanese bunkers **(1)** on Norfolk Ridge. It was these well built defensive positions that had held up the British advance along the foothills of Mount Pulebadze since 4th Brigade had swept down from above in early May, and where Captain John Randle of the Norfolks won his posthumous VC. It was difficult for commanders and staff officers who could not see the ground to understand how a small group of well-sited bunkers could hold up an advance until every single one – together with every single occupant – had been systematically destroyed. Japanese bunkers were formidable. Only the scarce medium artillery (the 5.5in. howitzers) could penetrate the roof; in fact, only direct and short-range sniping by Lee Grant tanks were guaranteed to defeat a Japanese bunker. Naga Hill **(2)** provides a backdrop to the scene to the north.

This bunker complex on GPT Ridge was much more substantial than the British had expected, with literally dozens of small, carefully sighted bunkers littering the entire area with interlocking arcs of fire, while the entire position was also

covered by Japanese machine guns further to the east on Aradura Spur.

No sooner would one be discovered and attacked, than another would open up against the attackers from somewhere else. Until the entirety of GPT Ridge was cleared, the road to Imphal remained in Japanese hands.

Here, the Royal Scots storm in on the bunkers under the direct fire support of the 75mm gun of the 28-ton Lee Grant tanks **(3)** of 150th Regiment RAC under the command of Major Ezra Rhodes, which had made their way past the recently captured Jail Hill and DIS Hill. The attack entailed getting very close, and rushing the bunker to detonate grenades and/or pole charges in any aperture available. The Royal Scots had by this stage been fighting non-stop since on 1 May they had crossed over Mount Pulebadze in an attempt to come on the GPT Ridge bunkers from above, and from an unexpected flank. Their approach march was a success, but the bunkers still required determined and individual treatment. With the destruction of the final Japanese positions on 14 May the way was opened up for the whole of 2nd Division to congregate in this area ready for the final assault on Aradura Spur, the next major ridge to the west, on 25 May.

British soldiers, possibly of the 7th Worcesters, fixing bayonets before advancing on Naga Hill. It is possible that this was preparation for the attack on Naga Hill (Point 5120) on 19 May. (IWM, MGH88/15)

edge of the hill. Here Hawkins had them dig to secure the ground that had been seized and the Worcesters, who had protected the flanks of the night advance, were called up to help build a defensive position able to resist counterattack. The rain was by now constant. Everyone was drenched to the skin. The next morning the Japanese Air Force made one of their occasional forays into the deep valley that flowed out of the Kohima Ridge westward, but to limited effect.

BACK ON THE PULEBADZE FLANK

Meanwhile, on the green slopes of Pulebadze on 6 May, B Company of the Norfolks, commanded by Captain Jack Randle, was ordered to seize the remaining part of the bunker position at the bottom of GPT Ridge, while the 4/1st Gurkhas of Brigadier Freddie Loftus-Tottenham's newly arrived 33rd Indian Brigade (which had begun to replace the battered British 6th Brigade on Kohima Ridge, having arrived by Dakota from Arakan between 5 and 9 April), assisting the breakthrough in the centre against Kohima Ridge and Jail Hill, were to attack the lower, western slopes of GPT Ridge. In these attacks the Norfolks were to seize the remaining Japanese bunkers but at high cost, in which Capt. Randle was awarded the posthumous VC. The Norfolks remained in the positions they had seized and, after a night of heavy rain, a further attempt to attack the remaining Japanese positions was made at first light on the morning of 7 May by the 4/1st Gurkhas and the Royal Scots. It was important that this operation was successful, as at 10.30am an attempt was to be made by the 1st Queen's – part of 33rd Indian Brigade, who had arrived at Kohima exhausted and malaria-ridden from Arakan the day before – on Jail Hill. If the machine-gun nests on GPT Ridge could be wiped out *before* the Queen's attacked they would enjoy a much higher chance of success. The only achievement on GPT Ridge that day, however, was bloody stalemate, with both

A mule train moving through the Traffic Control Point (TCP) after its capture. The TCP is the point at which the road to Imphal bifurcates – one part leading around the eastern edge of the Kohima Ridge and climbing in the direction of Jail Hill and GPT Ridge, and the other heading across Treasury Hill, through Kohima town and up onto Naga Hill. The monsoon rains are clearly evident. (IWM, MGH88/17)

Lieutenant-Colonel Hedderwick of 4/1st Gurkhas and Brig. Goschen being shot dead by snipers. The Queen's, aware that 4th Brigade had not managed to secure GPT Ridge, nevertheless went in against Jail Hill as planned and were slaughtered. In retrospect the attack was premature, but Stopford continued to demand speed to remove the Japanese stranglehold on Kohima in order to relieve beleaguered Imphal.

There was a belief in some higher quarters – held in particular by those whose only experience of the terrain came from reading a map in the comfort of a headquarters tent in the rear – that 2nd Division's offensive lacked pace. These accusations were preposterous to the hard-pressed men on the ground. It was impossible for commanders and staff officers in the rear who could not see the ground to understand how a small piece of jungle-topped hillside could absorb the best part of a brigade; how a small group of well-sited bunkers could hold up an advance until every single one – together with every single occupant – had been systematically destroyed; how only medium artillery (the 5.5in. howitzers) could penetrate the roof of a Japanese trench; how only direct and short-range sniping by Lee Grant tanks was guaranteed to defeat a Japanese bunker; how the desperate terrain, incessant rain and humidity led even the fittest men to tire quickly and what an extraordinarily determined opponent they faced. With few exceptions, the Japanese gave in only when they were dead. Every conscious man who could lift a weapon fought until he collapsed.

Attempts by 1st Queen's to secure Jail Hill on 7 May likewise failed. The British inability to break Sato's stranglehold was profoundly depressing for the men. After 34 days of some of the toughest fighting experienced anywhere during World War II the Japanese still held all the key ground, together with all of that, and more, that they had seized since 4 April. British morale was edging lower as the men struggled to contemplate how the intransigent Japanese might be moved from their bunkers. The Japanese feat of arms at Kohima was a miracle of defensive tenacity rarely matched anywhere else in the annals of war. Despite their lack of supplies Sato's troops dug themselves in with skill and imagination, ensuring that each bunker was mutually supported. Sato's defensive technique, while it was not going to enable him to break through Kohima by dint of offensive action, was designed to do the next best thing: to draw the enemy onto defences of great complexity and depth and to break them there, both physically and morally. In so doing his troops had to withstand the sort of conditions few other soldiers in history could have survived. They did so, and very nearly succeeded in persuading Stopford that battering through Kohima was an impossible task. Between the 4th and the 'Black 7th', for instance, the 38 3.7in. mountain guns dug in around Jotsoma fired over 3,000 rounds, the 48 25-pdrs fired over 7,000 rounds and the big 5.5in. guns of the medium artillery fired more than 1,500 shells at the Japanese positions, not to mention the almost continuous salvoes from the 3in. mortars of the infantry battalions and the constant strafing and bombing by Hurricanes and Vengeance dive-bombers. In spite of this almost endless torrent of fire and steel, Sato's troops continued to fight back doggedly and skilfully, boasting little more than their courage and resolve as, with virtually no air support, only a few artillery pieces and anti-tank guns, they repeatedly kept even the most determined British attacks at bay. Their strength of mind and willingness to fight to the death demonstrated the highest physical and moral courage and won the grudging admiration of their enemies.

In the weeks that followed, 5th Brigade on the left flank, 6th Brigade on Garrison Hill, 33rd Indian Brigade on the southernmost slopes of the Kohima Ridge, and 4th Brigade (now under the command of Robert Scott of the Norfolks after Brigadier Theobalds, Goschen's successor, was himself mortally wounded), ate away slowly at the Japanese defences. Nowhere were sudden gains made, but by gradual perseverance and the application of focused firepower the Japanese were destroyed, bunker by bunker, trench by trench. Rarely did the Japanese run, or retreat, remaining to die where they fought. The fighting was so close, so intense, that bullets were no respecter of rank. The 2nd Division lost four brigadiers in the Kohima battle, two killed and two wounded.

Men of C Company, 4/1st Gurkha Rifles, moving up after their successful attack on Jail Hill on the morning of 11 May. At 5am, following a 20-minute artillery bombardment, the Queen's rushed the first bunkers and within the hour had reached the summit, isolating and grenading each bunker one by one. (IWM, MGH88/19)

ABOVE
A soldier of C Company, 4/1st Gurkha Rifles, on the site of their success at Jail Hill. The same day the remainder of the battalion had helped clear DIS Hill. (IWM, MGH88/20)

TOP
Men of 4/1st Gurkha Rifles and 1st Queen's congregate on Jail Hill following its capture on 11 May 1944. (IWM, MGH88/21)

But British progress, though slow, remained sure, even though it seemed to the troops on the ground as if this battle would go on for ever. 4th Brigade cleared GPT Ridge on 11 May, by which time further costly attacks by the British 6th and 33rd Indian Brigades had finally forced the Japanese to relinquish their hold on Pimple, FSD and Jail hills, the latter of which was captured by the Queen's and C Company, 4/1st Gurkha Rifles. The tide was slowly – and painfully – beginning to turn. On the days that followed, the positions seized on 11 and 12 May were carefully consolidated, the remaining Japanese being exterminated one by one, sniper by sniper and gun by gun. No one could ever assume that a position was fully cleared until every body, every trench, every clump of undergrowth or pile of rubbish had been painstakingly checked over as sometimes, days after a position had been apparently 'captured', a corpse in his foxhole might pop up and fire off his last remaining rounds or throw a grenade at an unsuspecting soldier. The Berkshires cleared FSD Hill on 12 May, discovering that the Japanese had honeycombed the hill with tunnels, creating an elaborate underground fortress that included a battalion headquarters, repair shop, ammunition storage dump and hospital. Those Japanese bunkers on the western edge of the ridge that remained out of reach of the British artillery could now be engaged directly and at point-blank range by the Lee Grants, trundling up the road that divides DIS and Jail hills. They did so to the cheers of the British and Indian infantry, who found themselves hugging the ground as the 75mm smashed the enemy foxholes only metres from them, the ground shaking and the shockwave of the blast sucking out their breath and showering them with dirt and debris.

Operations of 23rd LRP Brigade north and north-west of Kohima, April–June 1944

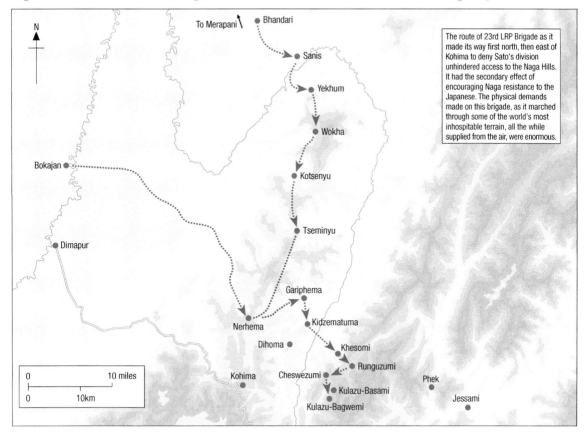

On the northernmost edge of Kohima Ridge on 13 May the sorely depleted Dorsets finally captured the smouldering remains of Pawsey's bungalow. On that day a final attempt to get a Lee Grant onto the tennis court succeeded. The tanks of the 150th Regiment RAC under the command of Major Ezra Rhodes were accompanied and protected by men of the Dorsets, fire from the lumbering leviathans allowing the infantry to close with the bunkers.

The capture of the southern end of the Kohima Ridge a full 37 days after the first arrival of Sato's men enabled Rhodes' Lee Grant tanks finally to trundle their way around the road and to use their guns against the remaining bunkers on the lower slopes of both Pimple Hill and GPT Ridge. The Norfolk Bunker, which had cost the life of the gallant Jack Randle, was finally taken by the Royal Scots with support from the tanks. Then, on 15 May, patrols from 5th Brigade moved down from Naga Hill, secured Treasury Hill and met up with the victors of Kohima Ridge on the Imphal road.

The capture of the Kohima Ridge was a remarkable triumph for the men of the British 2nd and the 7th Indian Divisions, following those who had held on so grimly under Richards' command at the start of the siege. But across the rest of the Kohima area lay a string of other Japanese positions, all of which remained to be eliminated; there was never any expectation that they might surrender, and they needed to be cleared by hand, inch by inch. Two principal redoubts remained: Point 5120 on Naga Hill and the Aradura Spur, the last remaining barrier on the road to Imphal.

Major-General John 'Black Jack' Grover, GOC of the British 2nd Division, shaking hands with a tank crew at Milestone 109 when the advancing forces from Kohima finally met up with the besieged Imphal Garrison, on 22 June 1944. (IWM, HU 2350)

BACK ON THE NAGA HILL FLANK

5th Brigade, now under the command of Brigadier Mike West, was preparing to launch coordinated set-piece attacks on the remaining, intransigent Japanese positions on Naga Hill (Point 5120) on 19 May. Previous attempts had failed. An attack by the Cameron Highlanders on Hunter's Hill on the night of 15 May was hurled back. In preparation for this attack bulldozers were used to cut a track up Naga Hill for the tanks. However, by this stage the desperate shortage of ammunition meant that the infantry would have to assault with little artillery support.

When, at 8.15am on Friday 19 May the attack went in; it was again repulsed. The weather was too poor for the promised air support, and the Japanese bunkers were laid out in considerable depth. When the Worcesters had taken eight bunkers they were faced with devastating fire from a further unheralded group of bunkers on the reverse slope that the artillery could not touch.

THE FINAL PUSH

Lieutenant-General Montagu Stopford now reorganized his forces in an attempt to maintain the greatest possible pressure on the Japanese. On 23 May Major-General Messervy's 7th Indian Division took responsibility for what had been 5th Brigade's area of operations on the left flank, the 4/15th Punjab, Queen's and 4/1st Gurkhas withdrew from the scene of their triumph on DIS and Jail hills to see what they might be able to do with the otherwise unbending defenders of Hunter's Hill. This switch allowed Grover to concentrate the remainder of his tired division for an attack on the Japanese positions on Aradura Spur. Both sets of attacks, first on Japanese defences around Point 5120 (Church Knoll and Hunter's Hill) by Messervy's 7th Indian Division on the left of the battlefield, and then of Aradura Spur by Grover's 2nd Division on the right, turned out to be miserable failures. On Naga Hill heavy attacks by Hurribombers were made from the air during the 24th and 25th, but the Japanese remained firmly entrenched and resolutely immovable. The proud

4/15th Punjab suffered a bloody reverse in these assaults, losing 18 officers and 443 casualties for not a single metre of ground in return. No combination of attacks from the air, artillery strikes, tanks, flame-throwers, infantry or mortars could shift Sato's men. Nothing seemed to be working, the troops were tiring and their morale – as a result of repeated failure to break the most stubborn defences imaginable – was plummeting.

The Japanese were, however, at this time beginning to recognize the limits of their own endurance. They were utterly exhausted and holding on grimly by the skin of their teeth. On 23 May Sato in an exhortation entirely unimaginable to a British army, had ordered his men: 'You will fight to the death. When you are killed you will fight on with your spirit.' But by now Sato realized that he was not going to be able to force the British from Kohima, or even to hold on indefinitely to what little he had gained. On 25 May he sent a signal to Mutaguchi which veiled an appeal to allow him to withdraw what remained of his division on the premise that it had run out of rations and the effect of the heavy monsoon rains required it 'to move to a point where he could receive supplies by 1st June at the latest'. Mutaguchi refused, ordering Sato to hold on for a further ten days.

THE LAST JAPANESE BASTIONS

Sato's final defence of Kohima was based on holding the two remaining bastions, one on Aradura Spur to the extreme right and the other on Hunter's Hill to the left. His last chance was that the British would exhaust and demoralize themselves in repeated attacks on positions that they had not demonstrated any propensity thus far to penetrate, let alone overcome. The British could not simply ignore Sato's bastions, nor could they be bypassed if the road to Imphal was to be reached and used to bring relief to the beleaguered IV Corps. Accordingly Grover ordered simultaneous assaults on both to take place on 27 and 28 May. On the right the Royal Scots and Norfolks were to attack the north-east end of Aradura Spur, while 6th Brigade were to take the south-west, where their objectives were named 'Matthew', 'Mark', 'Luke' and 'John'. When launched, however, 6th Brigade's attack on 28 May failed miserably. The weather was poor, the terrain atrocious and the morale of the exhausted 2nd Division the lowest it had been since its arrival. The obstinate Japanese just did not know when they were beaten, and British soldiers begrudged having to lay down their lives merely to teach them this lesson. The attack by the Norfolks and the Royal Scots on the north-west spur met the same fate as the luckless 6th Brigade. The Norfolks were now down to 14 officers and 366 men, many exhausted and ill and, despite the remarkable leadership of Lt. Col. Robert Scott and above-average morale, the Japanese positions looked typically impervious to anything other than a direct tank round into each bunker, which of course was not possible in the steep, jungle-matted hillsides. The attack was called off and the brigade withdrew, bringing its wounded with it. It is no understatement to say that the failure of the 2nd Division to secure the Aradura Spur was perhaps the lowest point of the long battle for Kohima. Yet again the Japanese had demonstrated their immovability, defying the odds despite their increasing weakness. The British troops were wet, exhausted and some units reduced to skeleton numbers while in at least one other, the Welch Fusiliers, morale had reached the point at which Brig. Shapland was forced to remove the commanding officer.

Operations to clear the road to Imphal

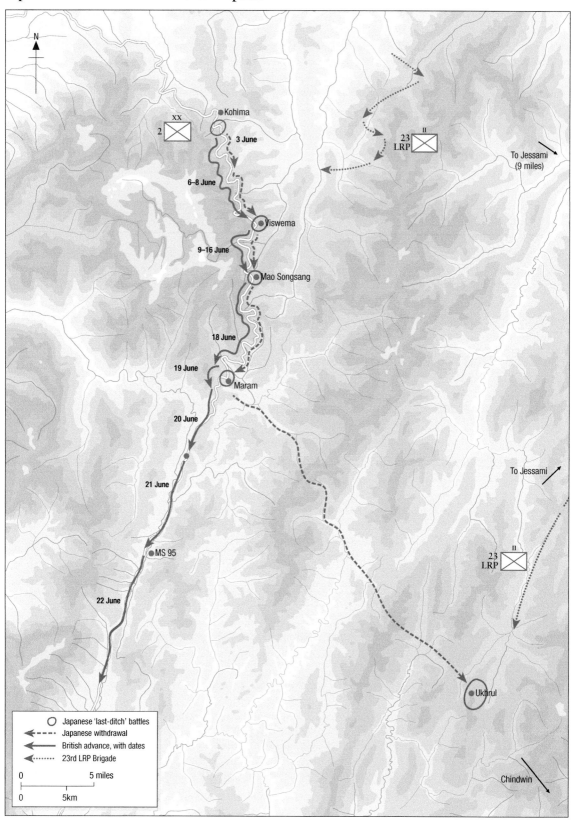

Legend:
- ○ Japanese 'last-ditch' battles
- ◄--- Japanese withdrawal
- ◄— British advance, with dates
- ◄····· 23rd LRP Brigade

0 — 5 miles
0 — 5km

Map labels: Kohima, 3 June, 6–8 June, Viswema, 9–16 June, Mao Songsang, 18 June, 19 June, Maram, 20 June, 21 June, MS 95, 22 June, Ukhrul, To Jessami (9 miles), To Jessami, Chindwin, 23 LRP, 2

Meanwhile, on the left flank 33rd Indian Brigade had not managed to find a way to break the Japanese defence of Point 5120. Stalemate once more threatened. Until, that is, the newly appointed 27-year-old commanding officer of the 4/1st Gurkhas – Lieutenant-Colonel Derek Horsford – decided to do things slightly differently, capturing Gun Spur at the extreme eastern edge of Naga Hill by a night infiltration on 27 May that took the Japanese entirely by surprise. This allowed tanks to approach the Japanese positions and, by 1 June, an attack by the Queen's discovered that the Japanese were pulling back.

THE COLLAPSE OF THE 31ST DIVISION

Sato's sense of alienation from the HQ of Fifteenth Army had not diminished during May. He was in no doubt that it was Mutaguchi's abject failure to send supplies through the mountains that had forced him to undertake the kind of passive defence in which his division was now engaged, preventing him from continuing offensive operations. Waiting in vain for any positive communication from Tamu, to where Mutaguchi had finally taken his HQ, four days later Sato reported that the position was hopeless, and that he reserved the right to act on his own initiative and withdraw when he felt that it was necessary to do so, in order to save what remained of his battered division from inevitable destruction. In fact, later that day he signalled Mutaguchi: 'We have fought for two months with the utmost courage, and have reached the limits of human fortitude. Our swords are broken and our arrows spent. Shedding bitter tears, I now leave Kohima.'

Apoplectic with rage and astonished at his subordinate's blatant disobedience, Mutaguchi ordered Sato to stay where he was. Sato ignored him and on receipt of Mutaguchi's threat to court-martial him, replied defiantly: 'Do as you please. I will bring you down with me.' The angry exchange continued, with Sato the following day sending a final angry message to Mutaguchi in which he declared: 'The tactical ability of the Fifteenth Army staff lies below that of cadets.' Sato then ordered his staff to close down the radio sets. The die was cast. Mutaguchi or no, he now began a fighting withdrawal with the remnants of his division.

Ignorant of Sato's dilemma, but harried by Stopford (and Slim's) urgent demands to make progress towards Imphal, Grover thrust troops from the newly captured Naga Hill south-east across the valley that runs east of the Kohima Ridge to seize a series of prominent ridges – Dyer Hill, Pimple and Big Tree Hill – to outflank Miyazaki's rearguard from 124th Regiment on Aradura Spur and to bring the 2nd Division's embarrassment to an end. Now, the Aradura Spur was itself cut off and Sato, recognizing the inevitable, began to withdraw south on 4 June.

The battle for Kohima could now be said to be over, although the road stretching down to besieged Imphal now needed to be peeled open. As if to signify the turn in British fortunes on 6 June news swept the division of the landings in Normandy. More importantly, the sun broke through the clouds and bathed the weary warriors below in the warmth of its embrace.

Comparatively rapid progress was achieved down from the hills on the Imphal road between 17 and 22 June once the Camerons and Worcesters had fought through the final obstinate defences at Maram and Viswema. The route was a defensive paradise on which an army any stronger than Sato's ragged, starving and emaciated troops could conceivably have held up the British advance indefinitely. Sato's rearguard fought determinedly. Often a few men with an artillery piece, grenades and a machine gun would take up positions on the high ground above tracks, ambushing the British advance guards before melting away to repeat the performance a few kilometres further back or, as was often the case, remaining obstinately in their positions until they were killed. Few were free from disease and fatigue, but surrender played no part in these men's vocabulary; they fought on till overtaken by a British bullet or bayonet or, more often, by starvation and exhaustion. But the 31st Division had literally fought itself to death. Exhausted men lay in pits unable to defend themselves, suicide squads with anti-tank mines tottered towards the advancing Lee Grants and Stuarts to be mown down by accompanying infantry, or obliterated by shellfire. The advancing troops now had their tails up; the Japanese blocks at Viswema and then Maram were swept aside with a fraction of the time and effort, and a tiny proportion of the blood and treasure, that had been expended in overcoming the Japanese defences at Kohima. All of a sudden the war, or at least the long struggle to defeat the thrust against Kohima, appeared to be nearing its end. Then, on Thursday 22 June a final surge linked the men of the 2nd Division with the defenders of the Imphal pocket. At Milestone 108 Captain Sean Kelly of the Durhams saw the tanks accompanying the advance guard of his battalion identify approaching troops of the 5th Indian Division. 'We sat alone in the sunshine and smoked and ate. Soon the staff cars came pouring both ways. The road was open. It was a lovely day.' The most desperate and bloody struggle in the entire war on the south Asian land mass had ended. It had lasted 79 days, had seen some of the most obdurate fighting of the war and cost the British around 4,000 men and the Japanese over 7,000 casualties.

AFTERMATH

By the time that Sato's rearguards were pushed back from Viswema in mid-June 1944 the entire Operation C was near collapse. It was only on 20 July, formalizing what was already happening to his shattered army, that Mutaguchi ordered a general retreat across the Chindwin. At the same time Slim ordered Stopford and Scoones to pursue Mutaguchi with such vigour that Fifteenth Army's defeat was turned into a rout. But the conditions conspired against a rapid British counteroffensive. Disease and malnutrition had weakened many and exhaustion was widespread. The extreme ruggedness of the terrain made progress difficult and slow. Many of Scoones' troops had fought continuously in appalling conditions for eight months. Nevertheless the 7th Indian Division pressed the 31st Division through the Naga Hills from the north-west, while elements of IV Corps moved north towards Ukhrul during June to cut the line of Japanese communication and withdrawal routes. Where they could the

'Chindits' from Brig. Perowne's 23rd LRP Brigade recovering in Dimapur after their three months of operations in the Naga Hills in support of XXXIII Corps. The months behind the Japanese lines in the Naga Hills formed a gruelling physical experience, in which all men lost considerable weight. (IWM, FLM 4076)

Operations of 23rd LRP Brigade in June–July 1944

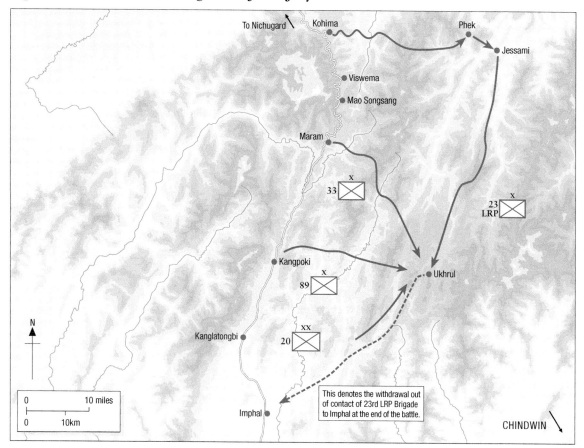

Japanese attempted to protect these routes by holding positions on the high ground but the experience for the few thousand remaining soldiers was a bitter one. Starvation, exhaustion and the savage monsoon rains daily extracted their toll, many hundreds dying on the endless, cloud-covered mountain ranges that flowed like angry waves on a mighty ocean all the way to the Chindwin. The pursuing British troops came across countless putrefying bodies, skeletons and abandoned weapons and material littering the jungle paths that led back through the hills to the Chindwin.

The advance towards Ukhrul and then the Chindwin was accompanied, far to the east, by part of Brig. Perowne's Chindit 23rd LRP Brigade marching deep into the Somra Tracts in an attempt to cut off the Japanese retreat to the Chindwin. It proved to be one of the most physically demanding challenges of the entire campaign.

The 33rd Brigade was ordered to give up their chase on 16 July, the evidence of profound Japanese defeat all around them, and their own troops weakening in the challenging conditions, causing Stopford to recognize that there was now little value in continuing the pursuit; the Japanese were a broken reed, and dying in vast numbers of their own accord, without the intervention of the British.

This advance proved to be the final chapter in the ignominious destruction of the Fifteenth Army. During July its entire command structure had disintegrated, men and units being left to fend for themselves in the life-and-

death struggle to evade the clutches of the slowly advancing Fourteenth Army; by the last day of July 1944 the battle for India could be said to be over. So perished Mutaguchi's army. Of the 65,000 fighting troops who set off across the Chindwin in early March 1944, 30,000 were killed in battle and a further 23,000 were wounded, a casualty rate of an unprecedented 81 per cent of combat forces, and 46 per cent of the total force involved. Seven thousand were lost at Kohima. Only 600 allowed themselves to be taken prisoner, most of them too sick even to take their own lives. Some 17,000 pack animals perished during the operation and not a single piece of heavy weaponry made it back to Burma.[1] The battle had provided the largest, most prolonged and most intense engagement with a Japanese army yet seen in the war. More importantly, for the British the collapse of Operation C and the retreat to the Chindwin created precisely the effect that was needed to contemplate an aggressive pursuit into Burma, and the overland recovery of Burma in 1945, long an elusive chimera in British strategy. Sato's defeat at Kohima was part of this overall failure, but distinguished from the ordinary first by Sato's refusal to obey Mutaguchi's order to advance on Dimapur and then, at the start of June 1944, his decision to withdraw the remnants of his starving forces from Kohima against the explicit orders of his superior commander, an act unprecedented in the history of modern Japanese command.

LEFT
A Japanese light tank, captured in good working order, being demonstrated after the battle. (IWM, FLM 4109)

RIGHT
Charles Pawsey introducing Mountbatten to Naga tribal leaders in Kohima, August 1944. Pawsey was one of the unsung heroes of the siege and subsequent battle. He remained on Kohima Ridge during the first phase of the battle, a tattered Union flag fluttering above his bunker. The Nagas remained completely loyal to him. Following the siege, and during the subsequent battle, Pawsey arranged for Nagas hiding in the hills to be brought to Jotsoma to be protected and fed. (IWM, FLM 4111)

1 The Fifteenth Army consisted of 115,000 troops, 50,000 of whom were support, line-of-communication and administrative troops. Of this number, 15,000 were lost, in addition to 53,000 fighting troops. The Fifteenth Army overall, therefore, lost 65,000 of its original strength.

THE BATTLEFIELD TODAY

Kohima is relatively easy to visit today, although certain restrictions apply, and permits to visit Nagaland are required. The modern Kohima is a straggling town of some 70,000, buildings now covering most of the areas where the fighting took place in 1944 in the higgledy-piggledy pattern of unplanned settlement. Nevertheless, the battlefield is easily discernable, at the heart of which lies the magnificent memorial on Garrison Hill. One of the first and best vantage points for the modern traveller is the hill at Zubza overlooking the road from Dimapur, and looking up the valley to see Kohima Ridge eight miles in the distance. On the left-hand side and on the other side of the Zubza nulla lies Merema, which the Japanese occupied in April 1944. At Zubza the Japanese were cleared from the road by the advancing 2nd Division.

The road then winds up the right-hand side of the valley, in the shadow of Mount Pulebadze on the far right of Kohima itself, before creeping around the IGH Spur (still the site of the Kohima Hospital) to the bifurcation of the road at the TCP. Immediately on the right, high above the road, sits the beautiful Commonwealth War Graves Cemetery and the 2nd Division

The battlefield today. This photograph looks from the tennis court south-west towards Aradura Spur, now the site of the Roman Catholic cathedral (out of site). The large white building behind the tree is the police station, perched on the top of Jail Hill. (Author's collection)

memorial with the famous words quoted at the front of this book. Few cemeteries evoke the sort of emotional power as that on the site of Garrison Hill, the famous tennis court and site of Charles Pawsey's bungalow. It was here that thousands of British, Indian and Gurkha dead (there are no Japanese cemeteries in India) lie for ever, their graves testimony to the sacrifice they made in holding this extraordinarily vital piece of terrain – the gateway to India – from the Japanese in 1944. It is possible, with assistance, to walk around most of Kohima Ridge, visiting the sites of Kuki Piquet, Jail Hill, DIS Hill and GPR ridge, amongst others. The Kohima Educational Trust (www.kohimaeducationaltrust.net), set up by veterans of the 2nd Division to pay tribute to the Naga people for their unstinting support during the battle, and which today supports the education of Naga children, has published an excellent guide to the battlefield. It shows among other locations the Aradura Spur, now the site of the Kohima Cathedral, and the positions around Naga Hill, such as Church Knoll and Hunter's Hill, where both 5th Brigade and the 7th Indian Division battled for so long to seize from a resourceful, formidable enemy. The guide is available free of charge, along with copies of newsletters and a leaflet describing the KET, from the trust's secretariat at 5 Beechwood Drive, Marlow, SL7 2DH, UK.

The Kohima authorities have established an excellent 'War Museum' some miles east along the Imphal road, which is worth a visit, and which will certainly improve over time as the volume of exhibits grows.

The best way to secure accommodation in Kohima, apart from staying in the single hotel, is to talk to a local. My favourite place is Asanuo's wonderful guest house (Razhü Pru) in Naga Village. Anyone making the trek to Kohima is encouraged to enjoy the warm hospitality of this old family home. The email address is razhupru@yahoo.co.in.

LEFT
The memorial to the British 2nd Division just above the busy TCP on the northernmost edge of the Commonwealth War Graves Commission Cemetery on Garrison Hill. (Author's collection)

RIGHT
'When you go home, tell them of us, and say, For your tomorrow, we gave our today.' Two reflective members of the Royal West Kents at the grave of Harman VC, after the battle. (IWM, IND 04886)

FURTHER READING

Allen, Louis, *Burma, the Longest War* Dent: London, 1984

Barker, A. J., *The March on Delhi* Faber and Faber: London, 1963

Campbell, Arthur, *The Siege, A Story from Kohima* Allen & Unwin: London, 1956

Colvin, John, *Not Ordinary Men* Leo Cooper: London, 1994

Edwards, Leslie, *Kohima: The Furthest Battle* The History Press: Stroud, 2009

Graham, Gordon, *The Trees Are All Young on Garrison Hill* Kohima Educational Trust: Marlow, 2006

Hart, Peter, *At the Sharp End: from Le Paradis to Kohima* Pen and Sword: Barnsley, 1998

Havers, Norman, *March On! An infantry battalion in England, India and Burma* Square One Publications: Worcester, 1992

Keane, Fergal, *Road of Bones* HarperCollins: London, 2010

Latimer, Jon, *Burma: The Forgotten War* John Murray: London, 2005

Lyman, Robert, *Slim, Master of War* Constable: London, 2004

——, *The Generals. From Defeat to Victory: Leadership in Asia 1941–45* Constable: London, 2008

Lowry, Michael, *An Infantry Commander in Arakan and Kohima* Gale and Polden: Aldershot, 1950

——, *Fighting through to Kohima* Leo Cooper: Barnsley, 2003

McCann, John, *Echoes of Kohima* self-published: Oldham, 1989

McLynn, Frank, *The Burma Campaign, Disaster into Triumph 1942–45* Bodley Head: London, 2010

Philips, C. E. Lucas, *Springboard to Victory: Battle for Kohima* Heinemann: London, 1966

Randle, John, *Battle Tales from Burma* Pen and Sword: Barnsley, 2004

Seaman, Harry, *The Battle at Sangshak* Leo Cooper: London, 1989

Shipster, John, *Mist Over the Rice Fields* Pen and Sword: Barnsley, 2000

Slim, William J., *Defeat into Victory* Cassells: London, 1956

Street, Robert, *The Siege of Kohima* Barney Books: Grantham, 2003

Tamayama, Kazuo, and Nunneley, John, *Tales by Japanese Soldiers of the Burma Campaign 1942–45* Cassell: London, 2000

Thompson, Julian, *The Imperial War Museum Book of the War in Burma 1942–1945* Pan: London, 2002

INDEX